FOR
WHITES
ONLY

FOR WHITES ONLY

REVISED EDITION

BY

ROBERT W. TERRY

WILLIAM B. EERDMANS PUBLISHING COMPANY
GRAND RAPIDS, MICHIGAN

Second edition, second printing, April 1977

ISBN 0-8028-1332-1

To

Douglass Fitch,

a black man
who confronted me with my whiteness
and challenged me to come to terms with it.

ACKNOWLEDGMENTS

This book represents the combined insights and struggles of many people. I especially want to express appreciation to the members of the Detroit Industrial Mission Staff, who continually encouraged me; Mr. David Wiley, who assisted on style and form; and my wife Jo-Ann, who supported the effort, contributed valuable insight, and compiled most of the selected bibliography.

CONTENTS

PREFACE TO THE REVISED EDITION

Written soon after the urban rebellions of the late 1960s, this book outlined an interpretation of the racial crisis for confused whites. In broad strokes, it proposed an orientation and style of action for those "new" color-conscious whites who sought creative roles in the struggle against racism and for fundamental justice.

The "new white consciousness" (NWC) proposal which the book advances was preliminary and tentative. There had been minimum testing of the the ideas themselves and little opportunity to put the concept into practice. With the passage of time, I have found an encouraging and surprising response to the book and its ideas. Thousands of whites from across the United States and many people internationally have responded positively. The book has also received support from blacks, Chicanos, native Americans, Asians, and others oppressed by a racist system. Reports have been received describing the initiation of new action projects or the redirection of existing projects because of the text.

An increasing number of whites have begun to realize that racial exclusion and exploitation on the one hand and coerced assimilation on the other are both racist. These two extremes set a precarious context for anti-racist work. The effort to find ways to attack these two faces of oppression seems to exceed America's wisdom and will. Whether it be an assault on the Black Panthers, massive one-way busing programs, or underdeveloped policies toward Third World countries, society's attempts at the practice of racial justice are wanting at best. Those commentators who blithely report the decline of racism in America should examine critically the standards and facts being used to measure success.

Liberals and conservatives alike are publicly acknowledging the limits of proposals they made during the 1960s.

A recent Ford Foundation study on race and ethnicity, for example, sought to answer the following question: "What factors, processes, and structures assist individuals and groups to perceive and relate to groups with whom they do not ethnically identify, with the same ethics, trust, justice, and other behavior associated to people with whom they do identify?" After a large number of regional conferences, involving a wide cross-section of experts of all races, a document was produced that was more striking by what it showed was *not* known than what was known.

The events of the 1960s and 1970s have shattered too many illusions about the American experience for any of us to rest easily with facile rhetoric or tired proposals. This is a sober time, a time to get to root causes and seek profound and far-reaching solutions. Peril and promise set the perimeters of the age. Ironically, the American bicentennial celebration comes just at the point where some important decisions have to be made so that America can avoid the peril and fulfil the promise of justice to all its citizens.

*   *   *

Much of *For Whites Only* I still affirm. Nationally, too few whites have self-consciously explored the meaning of whiteness. The desire to focus on blackness, particularly black pathology, or to probe into Latino, native American, or Asian problems is engrained in whites. Yet I have been encouraged when white groups who have to face their own whiteness move quite rapidly to fresh insight and creative action. I am more convinced than ever of the fruitfulness of approaching racism by way of examining white society rather than focusing on the victims. By starting with an examination of the oppressor and the oppressive system rather than the oppressed, whites can hear in new ways and with deeper appreciation what the oppressed are saying and doing.

One of the most gratifying aspects of *For Whites Only* has been the preliminary work done on values. Some anti-racists have attacked racism without clarifying their value base. This tends to make them narrow in their analysis of US society and provincial in forming various kinds of alliances with other groups experiencing oppression. I have found repeatedly that when groups begin to work on racism they are pressed back to their own fundamental orientation. Being anti-racist is not enough. Defining what we are *against* moves into clarifying what we are *for*. An increasing number of whites is being challenged to articulate alternatives to racism that go beyond simply its elimination. The urgent question that whites must answer is: What alternative models can replace the present American white-male-dominated society?

The concern for values encourages alliances with other groups who fight oppression, challenge institutional rigidity, demand access to resources, and battle cultural assimilation or exclusion. New whites cannot be anti-racist without also fighting against other forms of oppression. A firm value orientation identifies racism as one key denial of justice, but also points a way to identify other denials. Limitations of time may force us to choose priorities, but we cannot choose conflicting commitments and goals.

Collaboration rooted in pluralism rather than assimilation stems from these clarified values and provides a basis of workable relationship between people of color and whites. I proposed in *For Whites Only* that this kind of collaboration was possible. I did not sense as fully as I do now the pain in that collaboration, but I am still convinced of its long-term viability. One of the patterns that began to develop was that whites tended to announce they were "New Whites" and then expected oppressed people to cheer. In fact, we found that we were tested, pressed, checked out continually. Many whites whose orientation was traditionally liberal wanted trust first, then action. In fact, the reverse turned out to be a more realistic expectation. Only when whites developed battle scars of action and a willingness to match deeds with words were they trusted by people of color. Whites often tired of this continual testing, longing for the time when an easy relationship between groups would be possible. I see no escape from this kind of testing for many years to come. What I have found, though, is that, in spite of the testing, collaboration in fact becomes possible, common agendas are sets, and action does occur.

*   *   *

1

Some of the insights of the book have been changed and expanded over the past several years. I have shifted from exclusive use of a communication model, outlined in chapter two, to what I now call an active energy model. Much of the communication analysis remains but is now cast less in group and individual communication terms and more in terms of what is required for a society to become self-guiding. Amitai Etzioni's volume *The Active Society* (Free Press, 1968) has provided much of the theoretical base for this analysis. It has been tested and refined in my own work with large, complex organizations.

Whites coming to terms with a new white identity, being committed to personal and societal change, and risking actual change efforts must be coupled with an analysis of societal issues of power, culture, institutions, and resources. Not only must individuals change, society itself must be restructured. Too many whites want interpersonal solutions *apart from* societal changes. This desire is especially preeminent in groups working on improving human relations. But in fact both improved interpersonal relations and societal restructure are essential. The communication model tended to reinforce interpersonal solutions, even though that was not its intent nor is it a profound understanding of communication. Now I am struggling to find ways for whites to become increasingly active — self-aware, committed, risking — and build an active society that supports such new activity on the part of individuals and groups.

The definition I now use for racism flows from this shift in analysis:

> *Racism exists when one race/color group intentionally or unintentionally refuses to share power, distributes resources inequitably, maintains unresponsive and inflexible institutional policies, procedures, and practices, and imposes ethnocentric culture on any other race/color group for its supposed benefit, and justifies its actions by blaming the other race/color group.*

To be active a society requires equitable distribution of resources (equitable meaning distributed according to what is needed for each group to become active participants in society), shared power (not separate power), flexible and responsive policies, procedures, and practices, and a pluralistic culture (one that moves beyond superficial differences toward a serious wrestling with deeper values). Such a society will move in directions that generate the support and self-interest of all its citizens.

Such a society, of course, requires authentic communication among individuals and groups. It also requires a release and direction of active energy that is so structured that the whole society moves forward. How America directs itself, rather than becomes directed by ruling elites, internal and external economic forces, or cultural lag is the test of the next generation. It is the struggle in America to move from a white club to a just society.

Another shift following from the above comments has to do with what was during the 1960s the accepted distinction between individual and institutional racism. In *For Whites Only* I tried to include cultural racism as a third type of racism. However, as I continued to struggle with these distinctions, I have concluded that the appropriate fundamental categories are *societal* and *individual* racism. Societal racism includes the cultural, power, resource, and institutional dimensions implicit in any social context. "Societal" is a more comprehensive term than "institutional," which tends to focus too narrowly on institutional practices and policies. Given this new distinction, individual racism would be any individual action that perpetuates societal racism. Therefore, passive racism becomes a dominant form of racism in America. To do nothing is to perpetuate societal racism.

Although the book displayed the beginnings of a struggle to define the self-interest of whites in combating racism — especially the analysis of how liberals and conservatives contradict themselves because of their racist consciousness — this line of inquiry was not sufficiently developed. The more I have worked with whites on racism the more I realize the need to articulate clear self-interest arguments for whites combating racism. Whites need to understand more sharply how racism destroys them as well as others in the society.

3

Presently the self-interest argument divides into three lines. For some whites there is what might be called a normative self-interest in combating racism. Either we say the anti-racist struggle is right or we have personal religious or other normative convictions that carry us forward. Second, for a large number of whites there are the utilitarian self-interest arguments. Racism costs money. Property values go down, tax money needs to be diverted to problem areas that need not be problem areas, police forces have to be expanded. There is a body of literature that documents how the rise of racism costs the middle-income person much more money than it would if that racism were eliminated. The third line of anti-racist argument rests on simple coercion. Some whites feel that unless racism is eliminated the society itself will crumble. There is the direct fear that the perpetuation of a racist society will create the downfall for the whole society.

The necessity to stress self-interest is highlighted in the face of the claim made by some anti-racists that racism perpetuates "illegitimate white privilege." On the face of it this phrase seems valid and sensible. Whites do in fact benefit from racism in various ways, and those benefits, depending on skin privilege, are indeed illegitimate. But the problem with that phrase when used by itself without being coupled to a larger self-interest argument is that it leads to white guilt rather than a hard struggle with self-interest and change. If the only impact of white racism is seen as illegitimate white privilege, then the only argument for change is — stop being illegitimate! Such a fundamentally moral argument appeals to some whites but not to large numbers. And it casts even the moral argument into a negative posture rather than seeing the moral argument as a strength. That whites receive both privileges and penalties from racism is closer to the truth. The alternative I am suggesting here presses whites to realize that racism destroys white freedom as well as the freedom of people of color.

The final conviction that has been deepened since the writing of *For Whites Only* is that working on racism involves working for other broad changes in the society. In part, this is due to the value base underlying the new

4

color conscious proposal. As one becomes concerned about racial oppression, one also necessarily becomes involved with other forms of oppression. But this conviction is also related more directly to work on racism. Racism is frequently perpetrated intentionally. But it is also perpetrated as a by-product of other forces in the society. Joseph Barndt, in his volume *Liberating Our White Ghetto* (Augsburg, 1972), calls this correlate racism. According to Barndt, correlate racism takes place when "discrimination or other forms of minority exploitation occur as a by-product of policies or practices which in themselves are not racist. Correlate racism may take the form of a deliberate disguise to continue the oppression of minorities; or it may be a totally unintentional practice within an institution which is honestly seeking to be nondiscriminatory" (p. 61). I have found this concept very useful.

In some industries, for example, promotion from within the ranks of a given company is very satisfactory for employees in that company but serves as a quasi-seniority system to keep people of color at the bottom of the organizational hierarchy. Thus, we find that when we deal with the institutional character of racism, we have to attend to policies and practices that are not intentionally created to maintain oppressive racial patterns but in fact do so.

We have also learned in consulting with large organizations that practices and policies that have no direct bearing on race are often themselves oppressive to everyone. There may be, for example, poor performance review procedures for everyone. Thus, simply to include people of color in that institutional structure without changing the performance review practices means that we have included a new work force into a bad work situation. Consequently, much of the consulting I do necessarily combines a new color conscious advocacy with the best in general organizational change methodologies. The sacrifice of either of those aspects makes our work much less effective.

*   *   *

Now let me mention a few of the problems that have occurred since the writing of *For Whites Only*. One of the fears in producing such a book was that it could be misused to perpetuate rather than combat racism. Although I have tried to minimize these dangers, I have heard stories of the very behavior it was trying to eliminate. Some people have taken the argument that "racism is a white problem" to excuse whites from working with people of color to solve it. I stated in the addendum "Traps for the New White" that "the white community is the root of the problem, but the whole community — white, black, red, brown, yellow — must be deeply involved in any solution." That warning was obviously not enough.

Whites working by themselves have ended up one more time making decisions that affected the destiny of other people without permitting them any participation in the decision making. The formula "whites work in the white community and blacks work in the black community" makes only limited sense when whites begin to explore what it means to work in the white community. If one is working on a private, family manner, that is one thing. But if a group of whites tries to deal with any of the major institutions in the white community—industry, hospitals, education—it will soon become apparent that these institutions directly affect the lives of oppressed people. Therefore, although the separatist language is easy to adopt in principle, the distinction in practice is at best unclear. All major white institutions in America have direct and usually negative consequences for the lives of people of color. And no oppressed groups in America are starting automobile companies or any other major industries to compete with white-dominated industry. Therefore, to assume that whites can work with whites in the white community without collaboration is naive. In many ways the rhetoric of separatism from the white side disguises racist behavior and, in fact, perpetuates white control.

Another danger of new white consciousness is that it has supported individualism. Some people have equated pluralism with "doing your own thing." Instead of understanding pluralism as the struggle around "the one and the many," they have allowed individualism to take over and stressed the notion of "the many." This emphasis on "doing your own thing" results in a tendency to avoid the hard struggles around priorities and the conflicts attendant to those struggles. From an anti-racist perspective this kind of individualism is counter-productive. The task before us is to build important collaborative links among whites and between whites and oppressed groups that can unite in common action. Individualism splinters that and does not really provide for concerted collective action.

A third danger in new white consciousness was insufficient directions toward new behavior. *For Whites Only* emphasized new kinds of analysis and did not give enough attention to particular forms of anti-racist behavior. General comments about strategy and tactics did not lead to more specific comments about new white conduct with other whites and new white conduct in a collaborative mode with oppressed groups.

We have learned in industrial consulting, for example, that special attention must be given to how whites and people of color work together with a predominantly white organization. First, there is the question of leadership. Throughout this book I have stressed racial collaboration in problem-solving and accomplishing tasks. However, there are times when collaboration is simply impossible, whether due to time pressures or for some other reason. In those cases minority leadership is decisive. Not only must whites learn to collaborate, we must also learn how to follow.

A second dimension of this collaboration is sharing information. For strategic reasons, working on racism in organizations often requires that people of color meet in racially separate sessions. As whites, we need to know enough of what is going on to make informed, strategic, collaborative decisions on key issues, but we do not need to know the details of another racial group's private meeting. Whites who become nervous or miffed about these sessions should recognize that we meet in such sessions regularly — board meetings, staff meetings, and at athletic clubs. Because of this power imbalance, people of color should have more information flowing toward them than flowing in the opposite direction. White leadership in organizations, seeking aggressive ways to include people of color in organizational life, should make sure that information which has an impact on minorities flows directly to them.

Both new leadership patterns and new information flow patterns challenge a liberal desire for equal sharing. These new patterns are strategically required by a racist situation that is not equal.

Finally, I must mention one idea that was not developed at all in *For Whites Only,* but which has played a greatly increased part in my own developing understanding of racism. This is the relationship between domestic and international racism. Since the writing of *For Whites Only,* I have learned through contact with white anti-racists in other countries that their main entry into dealing with racism arose from an international perspective and moved from that context to a domestic one. In contrast, most of us in the United States started domestically and have had to include the international context in our thinking. Partly because of the Vietnam War, partly because of the rapid rise of multinational corporations, we have been forced to face directly the issue of reinforcing racism overseas. In the future both international and domestic analyses of racism will have to be combined. Particularly, I am looking for ways in which Third World people overseas can strengthen us in America to deal with our own white liberation.

* * *

Racial progress has been uneven at best and is continually being judged by new standards. Looking back over the years since this book was written, I have a cautious optimism about the possibilities in attacking racism. The fragile hope that we can at least contain if not eliminate racism has been built on the new reality beginning to break into the consciousness of whites. Spurred on by the self-conscious black power advocates forcing whites out of the civil rights movement, the war in Indochina, the increasing fears of fascism and genocide at home, and the deepening economic crisis, whites are realizing the perilous condition of white American society.

In a more profound way than perhaps we have experienced in our lifetime, the fundamental question facing the white community is not what whites can do for people of color in some paternalistic way, but profoundly how can we build solidarity to liberate all of us from white racism.

Part of my cautious optimism is rooted in two facts that provide a basis for future action. The first is that America has in fact turned a corner in its dealing with oppressed people domestically and internationally. No longer can white America treat people of color with impunity. We could not do it in Vietnam, nor can we do it in America. Most capricious and arbitrary actions by local and federal governments are gone. There has been sufficient mobilization by people of color in this country to resist many of the gross forms of racism. This is not to say that selective attacks on people of color have become impossible: witness the treatment of Blacks in Boston. There is, however, a shift in power that needs to be strengthened rather than ignored.

Secondly, I am encouraged by the possibility of authentic though painful collaboration among whites and people of color. I am encouraged to find that where whites are seriously committed to both theory and practice of new white consciousness, new collaborative relationships occur.

Many of the activists of the 1960s recognize the limits of their own analysis of societal racism. A large number have returned to schools and universities with a level of urgency and questions that have challenged many of the traditional professorial answers. Others are moving into professions like law to seek new access to the levers that move institutions. Generally a more reflective stance has been taken, reflecting a realization of the inadequacies of dogma and the necessity to develop theory, assumptions, and analysis that are in keeping with particular changes in the American situation.

Action projects are becoming increasingly local because there is little confidence that any progressive leadership will issue from Washington. There is also fear of heavy repression if a national movement surfaces prematurely before a solid base can be assembled. However, there is a strong conviction that a national mobilization will eventually be built upon new collaborative relationships between people of color and whites.

The new organizing is more radical and comprehensive. It seeks to put together local alliances to attack America's problems at their roots—its racism, sexism, ecological exploitation, anti-Semitism, agism, and class oppression — and to construct workable alternatives. Some of this work is being done in separate social, sexual, and class groups; others express solidarity across such lines.

I have been deeply gratified that groups mobilizing in these new directions have found *For Whites Only* a useful resource in their efforts to effect change. Formal and informal networks established across the country maintain communication around these issues, and I sense that a new kind of movement may replace the civil rights movement as an energizer for societal change. This movement may not depend on marches and major public events for mobilization, but probably will involve intensive local work broadly coordinated through these national networks.

An image that sustains my cautious optimism was first stated by Amitai Etzioni. "Mobilization," he writes, "is usually not a mass situation in which a charismatic leader activates a large body ... more or less simultaneously, like a match set to gasoline. Rather, the process is similar to lighting heavy, damp wooden logs" (p. 405). My cautious optimism is built on the fact of many people lighting damp logs. Together we are working to light the fire for our common liberation.

Summer 1975   R. W. T.

INTRODUCTION

During recent years of racial upheaval, white America has made a series of concessions to demands by blacks. In spite of the victories won by black Americans from whites, however, there seems to be no cessation of black demands; instead of subsiding they are escalating. And from all present signs, there is no relaxation ahead. Whites, struggling to make sense out of the intensified racial conflict in this country, respond in diverse ways.

I. A WHITE QUANDARY: WHAT DO BLACKS WANT?

In response to growing demands, increasing numbers of white Americans fear there is no way to satisfy the black community. Whites seem to be in a no-win situation. Whatever they do is quickly interpreted by some blacks as inadequate, minimal, or racist. A few whites, trying not to be castigated by blacks, have made extra efforts to be sensitive to their real desires. They have found among blacks a unified demand for justice but conflicting interpretations of what justice is. Sensitive and concerned whites quickly realize that division within the black community prevents the placing of unified demands upon white-dominated political, economic, and social institutions.

Consequently, searching whites are in a quandary. They don't know how to read the desires of blacks and have lost what they thought was a sure guide to solving the racial crisis. Whites believe that if they could figure out what blacks want, satisfaction of those demands would cause the race problem to disappear. Instead, what whites are finding is a "damned if you do, damned if you don't" response from the black community.

A. Case in Point: Housing

If suburban whites push for open housing, they are damned because they offer too little too late. They are told

11

that blacks don't want to live in the suburbs anyway. If whites, reacting to this black response, try to justify racially separate communities, they are blasted as racists and bigots.

Many colleges recently have ruled that dormitories should be integrated. This had been a demand by blacks for years. Just as the order begins to be enforced, a group of black students resent the integration ruling and call for their own dormitory. College and university administrators are caught in the crossfire and thrown into a quandary: What is the appropriate campus policy? What do blacks really want?

B. Case in Point: Law Enforcement

If law enforcement programs are firmly administered, whites are damned because they are supporting a brutal, repressive system, unresponsive to the black community. But if firm law enforcement is not administered, blacks cry that police are not stamping out crime in the ghetto. This ambiguity was highlighted in a magazine article on police in the ghetto:

> For officers Letterman and Marre — indeed, for tens of thousands of white cops in tense urban ghettos across the land — there is no simple answer. They are caught up in the midst of an increasingly bitter debate over their powers, their conduct and their role in society. Many whites and middle-class Negroes, frightened by urban violence and the crime rate that is growing seven times as fast as the U. S. population, are clamoring for tougher law enforcement. At the same time, increasing numbers of black radicals, convinced that policemen value property over human life, order over social justice, are trying to strip them of their authority.[1]

C. Case in Point: Education

If whites push hard for a policy of integration and encourage mixing of racial groups by busing, redistricting, and other means, they are damned because they undermine local black control of black schools. On the other hand, if whites argue for local control, they are damned for rationalizing their racism under the guise of maintaining quality education. If the problems of local control and quality education

---

[1] Trevor Armbrister, "White Cops in the Black Ghetto," *Saturday Evening Post*, XXIII (November 1968), p. 27.

aren't sufficient grounds for conflict, the question of the role of teachers' unions compounds the difficulty. The same quandary faces whites: What do blacks want?

D. CASE IN POINT: INDUSTRY

If white managers hire hard-core blacks and develop extensive training programs for them, they are damned because they are opening unskilled and menial jobs — jobs with little future and almost no power. Then, if they automate or for any reason are forced to lay these men off, they are damned as socially irresponsible contributors to racial unrest. Detroit's automobile industry is frequently trapped between walls of conflicting criticisms. Automakers are in a quandary: what do blacks want?

While these examples are not exhaustive and don't portray all the complexities of the issues, they do illustrate conflicting interpretations of justice by the black community. However, it is these conflicts that deepen despair among whites trying to act constructively to alleviate racial turmoil. Frequently, in conversations with white people, we hear that factions within the black community are slowing racial advance. Blacks are fighting against themselves when they should be presenting unified demands for justice to the white power establishment. If blacks don't know what they want, how can whites respond appropriately?

II. A WHITE QUANDARY: WHAT ABOUT GROWING MILITANCY AND VIOLENCE IN THE BLACK COMMUNITY?

Many whites who think they understand the blacks are bewildered and openly angry when rejected, castigated, and confronted by articulate blacks with advanced black consciousness. Attitudes of mutual respect and tolerance, once thought to be solid, become shaky. Questions come from whites in rapid order: Why the black anger and hostility? Why the attacks? Why the growing militancy and violence in the black community? Aren't we making progress? Blacks are going too far with all their black power talk. Militancy will only be self-defeating for blacks. Martin Luther King's way was the proper way — nonviolence. That's the way to real racial progress.

A.   A Case in Point: UAW and DRUM

Recently the United Auto Workers distributed a policy letter to its local union offices. The letter was sent in response to increasing militancy on the part of a developing black organization — Detroit (or Dodge) Revolutionary Union Movement. In part, the letter stated:

> A group now exists in a few plants where UAW represents the workers which calls itself a black revolutionary movement and whose goals are the complete separation of the races in the shop and the destruction of the union through the tactics of violence, fear, and intimidation.
>
> The UAW, however, will not protect workers who resort to violence and intimidation with the conscious purpose of dividing our union along racial lines. . . .
>
> The establishment of black organizations to influence the destiny of black people in American society is a sound concept. Separatism, dividing society, instilling fear and hatred, using violence and intimidation, however, are divisive, harmful to the workers and their welfare and damaging to the basic democratic values of society.[2]

B.   Case in Point: White Citizenry and Black Power

For most white Americans, the slogan "black power" symbolizes growing black militancy like no other term. A study of the impact of the phrase on black and white confirms this educated guess.

According to a research study, almost 40 percent of whites believe black power means black rule over whites. Some typical responses sounded like this:

> Nasty word! That the blacks won't be satisfied until they get complete control of our country by force if necessary.
>
> Black take-over — take over the world because that is what they want to do and they will. There's no doubt about it. Why should they care? I'm working and supporting their kids. . . .[3]

When all the white responses were grouped by either positive or negative reactions to the black power slogan,

---

[2] The United Auto Workers International Executive Board, March 10, 1969.

[3] Joel Aberback and Jack Walker, "The Meanings of Black Power: A Comparison of White and Black Interpretations of a Political Slogan," unpublished manuscript, University of Michigan, 1968, p. 6.

14

only about 11 percent were at all positive. Most whites equated black power with black rule over white, black racism, trouble, or rioting. Eleven percent of the whites responded with ridicule, abhorrence, or outright obscenity.[4] What the study clearly shows is that most whites, even those who consider themselves "liberal" on the race issue, are threatened, bewildered, upset, and angry because of heightened militancy in the black community.

III. THE MISPLACED QUANDARIES

For years, whites have merely reacted to black demands and methods. While that approach may have been appropriate in the past, it is no longer possible. White concern about what blacks want is confounded by the absence of a unified black voice. White rejection of black militancy seems only to intensify the militancy.

The alternative to mere reaction requires a fundamental and far-reaching realization by whites. The strategic target for solution to the race question is wrong. The white quandaries are misplaced. *What is at stake for white America today is not what black people want and do but what white people stand for and do.* The racial problem in American society is not a "black problem." It is a "white problem." If there are racial ambiguities, conflicts, and contradictions in black America, it is only because these factors are deeper and more far-reaching in white America. The time has come to attack the causes of the racial crisis, not the victims. We must shift the locus of the problem from black to white. Frank Joyce, white leader of the national group People Against Racism, aptly captured our racial plight in a paraphrase of a famous military statement — "We have met the enemy, and they are *us.*"[5] This insight is part of what we would call *new white consciousness.*

It sounds relatively simple to shift target groups. At an intellectual level, it even makes sense to isolate the white community as the real problem. But it is not easy to make the shift, because we have been taught for too many years

---

[4] *Ibid.*

[5] Although this phrase originally appeared in a "Pogo" cartoon, it was appropriately used by Frank Joyce as the title of an unpublished paper on racism, circulated by People Against Racism (PAR).

that we have a black problem. Reorientation is difficult, even for the sophisticated white who recognizes the gross injustices perpetuated on blacks by whites.

This difficulty of shifting orientation is shown in the report of the National Advisory Commission on Civil Disorders (popularly known as the Kerner Report). The document clearly identifies the white community, particularly white institutions, as the root cause of racial problems. "What white Americans have never fully understood," the commission charges, "but what the Negro can never forget — is that white society is deeply implicated in the ghetto. White institutions created it, white institutions maintain it, and white society condones it."[6]

Among many remarkable features to the study, perhaps the most obvious is that it was written at all. Most important to remember is that it was not written by radicals, but by white and black moderates. Many members of the commission reported shock and agonizing surprise at what they found in America, and voiced deep concern that something be done about the white society that had created this racial monster.

The type of solution the commission proposed to the "white problem" can be seen in their statement on education:

> Education in a democratic society must equip children to develop their potential and to participate fully in American life. *For the community at large, the schools have discharged this responsibility well* [emphasis added], but for many minorities, and particularly for the children of the ghetto, the schools have failed to provide the educational experience which could have overcome the effects of discrimination and deprivation.[7]

The report makes clear the desire of the black community for better schooling and argues that "Negro students are falling further behind whites with each year of school completed."[8] Integration is supported as the priority educational

---

[6] *Report of the National Advisory Commission on Civil Disorders* (March 1968), p. 1.

[7] *Ibid.,* p. 10.

[8] *Ibid.,* p. 12.

strategy; but later the report states, "Equality of results with all-white schools must be the goal."[9]

Initially, this analysis seems acceptable and makes good sense. It appears appropriate to upgrade ghetto schools so they have quality education equivalent to the best white schools. But the report reveals a crippling contradiction. *While white institutions are indicted as the main cause of our racial problems, the same white institutions are used as the standard of success.* The solutions were designed to rid America of its black problem by making blacks white. Thus, a report that begins as a promising analysis of white racism fails to carry that analysis through to its necessary conclusion. For few, if any, programs were designed to modify or radically change the white-dominated institutions that determine and carry forth racial policies.

Awareness of this contradiction means, for whites who want to face white racism head on, that we begin to look at ourselves, our institutions, and our culture from a new perspective if we ever hope to solve the *real* race problem. We need to know the enemy much better before we begin the campaign and plan a victory celebration.

IV. PROPOSAL: NEW WHITE CONSCIOUSNESS

Is there a way out of the white quandaries? How can we find out who we are as white Americans, what we stand for, and what new kinds of actions are required? The answers to these questions point toward the development of men and women with a *new white consciousness:* an awareness of our whiteness and its role in race problems. A new white consciousness is essential inasmuch as other options seem to lead to dead ends or impossible solutions.

A. WHITES CANNOT BE COLOR-BLIND

The idea of new white consciousness has puzzled many people. A first impression for some is that it is a step backward rather than forward. The emphasis on color, they argue, only serves to perpetuate division. Instead of being color-conscious, we should be color-blind. We need a new *human* consciousness, not *white* consciousness. It is possible, they suggest, for a white and black man to relate authenti-

---

[9] *Ibid.*

cally, as human beings, in deep trust, without being blocked by the color issue.

This argument is often couched in highly moral terms and espoused from a wide spectrum of "radical to nonradical" perspectives. An example from a radical point of view was attributed to a white student in an interview with Eldridge Cleaver. The student is reported to have said:

> You are denying my humanity and my individuality. Though I am in deepest empathy with you and with all blacks — all people — in their struggle to be free, you are in danger of becoming my enemy. I must revolt against your racism, your scorn of everything white, just as I revolt against the racism of white America. I will not let you put me in a bag. Your enemies and my enemies are the same people, the same institutions. . . . I feel no special loyalty to White, but only Self. I feel no love for the leaders or institutions or culture of this country, but only for individual people, in an ever-growing number, with whom I share love and trust. I deny my whiteness; I affirm my humanity. You are urging your black brothers to see me only as White, in just the same way as we have been raised to see you only as Negro. . . . I don't feel white enough or guilty enough to die joyfully by a bullet from a black man's gun, crying "Absolved at last!" And I know that soon you, by denying me my me-ness will become for me just as much an oppressor, just as much an enemy, as the white culture we are both fighting. . . . To remain free, and to transform society, I have to maintain my hard-won differentiation from the mass of white people, and I won't let even a black person, no matter how hard-bent he be on black liberation, squeeze me back into honkie-dom. If I have to shoot a black racist one of these days, well, baby, that's part of the struggle.[10]

This student is struggling to be a new white, but he is misled on two counts: first, he thinks he can exonerate himself from being white by simply asserting that he is human, and second, he equates any mention of color with racism.

Protestations to deny whiteness eliminate neither the fact nor the problem of white privilege. American culture is

---

[10] "Playboy Interview: Eldridge Cleaver, A Candid Conversation with the Revolutionary Leader of the Black Panthers," *Playboy Magazine* (December 1968), p. 100.

color-conscious. We sort people by color, to the advantage
of some and detriment of others. To dissociate oneself from
whiteness by affirming humanness ignores what whiteness
has done and how we continue to benefit from it.

The equation "color consciousness equals racism" is also
misleading. As we shall see later, racism is not just the consciousness of color, but what is done with that consciousness.
To overlook that fact is to assume that the black experience and white experience in America are identical. Inasmuch as whites have been the perpetrators and beneficiaries
of white racism, however, their experience is markedly different from that of the black, who has been the victim.

One small way to test the difference in color consciousness is to ask whites and blacks when they first became
aware that whiteness was something with which they had
to deal. Only a few whites we have asked go back as far
as two or three years. Most have never considered being
white a problem. Just about all blacks, on the other hand,
with whom we have talked recall one vivid experience after
another of having to cope with whiteness, from early child-
hood on.

To assume so easily, as did the student, that any mention of color is racist disguises this fundamental difference.
The issue that the student missed is that color consciousness is a fact of life in America and that recognizing that
fact does not in itself make one a racist. Racism is not
color consciousness per se, but how that color consciousness is used by one people against another.

A more common example of trying to be color-blind
occurs when a white person remarks to a black, "I didn't
even think of you as a Negro." That person thinks he is
being color-blind. But the necessity of the statement gives
the lie to its supposed meaning. If color were not important,
we would not feel the need to comment on it. The white
could be trying to say one of two things. He might see the
Negro as being so close to white in color and manner that
the color "faded" in importance. If so, he is not being
color-blind but is absorbing blackness into whiteness. Or,
he could be trying to affirm that he doesn't discriminate on
the basis of color. If so, he is still not being color-blind, but

trying to find some way to articulate his concern for racial justice.

The Kerner Report documents that signs posted in many white, Christian churches are just not true:

> Democracy is color-blind
> Christianity is color-blind
> Are you?

If we seriously want to eliminate racial injustice in America, instead of pretending to ignore color we must be color-conscious in a radically new way.

B. WHITES CANNOT BE BLACK

Some whites, having recognized the futility of being indifferent to color, have taken another tack. They have identified with blacks so completely that they want to deny their own whiteness. They talk like blacks, dress like blacks, read mostly black literature, listen to black music, pick up most clues about what to think from blacks, and try, sometimes quite desperately, to get personal recognition from blacks for being "almost black." This group too gets caught short by the concept of new *white* consciousness. New whiteness challenges whites who attempt to live off black consciousness and black power. New whiteness questions the radical hate many of these whites have for whiteness. Whiteness cannot be denied by efforts to be black. Another foundation is required — a new white consciousness.

New white consciousness is a bridge concept. The *new* in the label points to fresh possibilities. We are not totally limited by our past. *White* is a constant reminder that we are not racially neutral, and also a reminder that we still participate in racist institutions and culture. *Consciousness* continually reminds us that we need to reconstruct totally our understanding of who we are and what we ought to do. New white consciousness, then, is a way for us to understand ourselves simultaneously as white racists and as creators of justice.

As new-conscious whites, we have at least six urgent tasks:

(1) Become conscious agents of change — recognize that new directions are possible.

(2) Seek ethical clarity — know what we ought to stand for and why.

20

(3) Identify the multiple forms and expressions of white racism — know who we are and have been, and why.

(4) Develop social strategies for change to eliminate and move beyond racism — experience what our society might be.

(5) Discern the appropriate tactics — assess our power for change.

(6) Experiment, test, and refine personal styles of life congruent with our newly affirmed values — experience who we might be.

These six tasks will form the skeleton for the remainder of this essay. We are at an exciting juncture in race relations. For perhaps the first time, we can see ourselves as the real problem and begin to deal with causes instead of symptoms. We can learn to affirm ourselves and others with a new depth, chart courses to take us beyond racism, and develop a quality of life fulfilling for all people.

CHAPTER I

NEW WHITE AS AGENT OF CHANGE

I. POSSIBILITY OF CHANGE

The first task for the new white is to recognize his potential as an agent of change. It does little good to be committed to the elimination of racism if we are socially impotent. Many people become excited about a particular change only to suffer a crisis of confidence; they fear they lack the power to effect the change. In particular instances they may be correct. People cannot always cause change at will. Sometimes, however, lurking in the background is the feeling that no significant social change is possible in a world so complex and overwhelming. Social processes and events are felt to be out of human control. If there is any control, it must be at the top, certainly not in the middle or at the bottom.

Until recently, social scientists offered little challenge to this pervasive sense of impotence. Self and society, they appeared to suggest, resulted from forces beyond human control. Regardless of whether the result of these forces was humanly beneficial, it was difficult to see human intervention as critical to historical change and development.[1]

Today, a notable shift is occurring in social theory. Amitai Etzioni, widely recognized scholar and Columbia University sociologist, in his most recent book *The Active Society* recovers an active view of the self. Men can initiate and sustain change, he argues, when acting in self-conscious groups. Men must abandon the myths of individual heroics

---

[1] For further development of this point see Amitai Etzioni, *The Active Society* (N.Y., The Free Press, 1968); and Gibson Winter, *Elements for a Social Ethic* (N.Y., Macmillan, 1966).

or of total captivity by "the system." There are other options. We can have a society that is master of the traditions and institutions it creates.[2] The decision clearly rests in the human community.

The effort by Etzioni and other social scientists to raise to the surface the question of man's potential for change has great implications for the new white. It says that even though we have been raised as racists, it is possible for us to identify that racism and surpass it. We are rooted in our past; we are not exhausted by it. We are finite; we are free.[3] We are never mere things nor are we ever merely isolated individuals. Rather we are selves in society, and potentially we are transformed selves in a changed society. For each of us, the future is open. It is not exhausted by the realities of the past. It awaits fundamental change. "Potentially," writes Etzioni, "every man is free to choose; social laws, unlike those of nature, can be flaunted and, above all, re-written."[4]

II. WHAT NEEDS CHANGING?

If white racism is the fundamental cause of racial upheaval in America, what must be changed to rid us of that racism? Usually the options are two — attitudes or behavior. For a long time bad white attitudes were understood as the block to good race relations. If attitudes were changed, appropriate behavior would follow. In this view, attitudes were pictured as the most basic determinants of action. Attitudes usually involve feelings, convictions, or moods toward individuals, groups, institutions, or things. Changes of be-

---

[2] Etzioni, p. vii.

[3] Merleau-Ponty, distinguished French philosopher, describes freedom as follows: "What then is freedom? To be born is both to be born of the world and to be born into the world. The world is already constituted, but also never completely constituted; in the first case we are acted upon, in the second we are open to an infinite number of possibilities. But this analysis is still abstract for we exist in both ways *at once*. There is, therefore, never determinism and never absolute choice. I am never a thing and never bare consciousness." *Phenomenology of Perception* (London, Routledge and Kegan Paul, 1962), p. 453. See also Calvin Schrag, "The Structure of Moral Experience: A Phenomenological and Existential Analysis," *Ethics,* LXXIII (July 1963); and Paul Tillich, "What Is Basic in Human Nature," *Pastoral Psychology,* XIV, 131 (February 1963).

[4] Etzioni, p. 2.

havior or action would follow changes of these feelings, convictions, or moods. If we could get whites to feel respect and be sincerely open to blacks, then justice would emerge.

The other option reversed the order, attempting to change attitudes by first changing behavior. Behavior, in this context, meant any outward observable action such as language, physical appearance, or other public expressions. Once behavior was changed, the argument went, then attitudinal change would follow. In industry, for example, rather than engage in interpersonal-awareness programs, which open the questions of feelings, convictions, and moods, some men are attempting to clarify and enforce company policy that specifies accountable behavior. The argument behind this move is based on the belief that blacks and whites when forced to work together in common tasks as peers undergo attitudinal change, occasioned by the new behavioral relationships.

Some companies are implementing a policy, for example, that prohibits use of any words of disrespect such as boy, nigger, and spick. The new behavioral expectations are buttressed by stiff penalties if violated. In this approach attitudes are not attacked directly. The only requirement is that attitudes conflicting with company policy must be kept private.

The debate rages on today. However, one critical arena of human experience has been ignored in the debate — consciousness. It is not enough to change white attitudes and white behavior. We must also change white consciousness. What does this mean?

To be conscious is to be always actively aware of ourselves in relation to selves and things around us. We are always in the process of "making sense" of our experiences, no matter how shattering, traumatic, or novel. If we momentarily lose our physical equilibrium, we know how much energy we expend trying to regain our balance. The same is true socially. If something strange or surprising occurs, we spend whatever energy is necessary to place the event in some perspective that "fits" other experiences we have had. Aron Gurwitsch, philosophy professor, states it well:

> Experience always presents us with objects, things, events, etc., within certain contexts . . . , and never with

isolated and scattered data and facts. Looking at a material thing, e.g., a book, we perceive it in certain surroundings. We see the table on which the book is lying, we see other books, papers, pencils, pipes, and through the window, a segment of scenery outside the house. Every material thing is perceived amidst other things which form a background for its appearance. Correspondingly, the same is true with regard to thinking. When we are dealing with some theoretical problem, more than the problem alone is given to consciousness. . . . Absorbed though our attention may be with the problem, we never lose sight of our actual surroundings nor of ourselves as situated in those surroundings.[5]

Our consciousness of ourselves in our surroundings provides a basic orientation that continually describes and evaluates what is happening. Through our consciousness we recognize that we are not identical to what is occurring but inextricably related to it.[6]

For most white Americans, the orientation used to interpret the racial situation has not understood whites to be the problem. We have been taught that America was the great melting pot and any blockage of blacks from entering the mainstream was not white unwillingness but black inability. Our old white orientation interprets blacks, not whites, as the problem. This is reinforced by conflicting black demands and increasing militancy. Blacks don't know what they want, the orientation tells us, and they are using immoral means to achieve whatever it is they are after.

To shift the whole issue around, to understand whites as the basic problem, is to change consciousness radically. It is an effort to create a new orientation, with the expectation that it will be a better way of understanding the present and a surer guide for future action.

Attitudes and behavior are critical, and both must be changed; but the attitudes will be misplaced and behavior misdirected if consciousness remains untouched. Attitudes and behavior are interdependent. They can reinforce or con-

[5] Aron Gurwitsch, *The Field of Consciousness* (Pittsburgh, Duquesne University Press, 1964), p. 1. See also William Luijpen, *Existential Phenomenology* (Pittsburgh, Duquesne University Press, 1960).

[6] See Luijpen, p. 107, especially the idea of distance as affirmation and negation of object perceived.

tradict each other. We neither always do as we feel nor have strong feelings about what we do. But in either case, the sense we make of our attitudes and behavior is dependent on the orientation we use. If it sees blacks as the problem, then both attitudes and behavior will flow from that definition of the situation. If, on the other hand, we become oriented so that we understand ourselves as the problem, then it becomes possible to explore new behavior and reevaluate earlier attitudes.

III. WHITE READINESS TO CHANGE

Change is usually resisted. Even minor changes of things people hold important are strongly resisted. Yet change can be introduced to both self and society when our usual understanding of events and situations is called into question. We have already suggested that historical events do not just happen. Events happen and are interpreted within some meaningful and usually nondoubted context.[7] Our attention is focused on doing particular things; little if any time is spent reflecting on the general context — who we are, the value of the task, or the likelihood of successful performance. Very few men with Chrysler, Ford, or General Motors spend much time questioning whether having a big production year is in the best interest of the company or the country. Most men assume without question the value of increased production. They orient their behavior and attitudes within that framework. Likewise we all develop lines of expectation, which become guidelines for our self-expression in the multidimensional context of the social world.

When, however, these patterned responses and expectations are ripped apart so that social benchmarks no longer offer secure guidance for the future, then men are vulnerable to change. As doubt intensifies, the need to make sense out of the new events heightens. People are ready for a new orientation.

---

[7] See Alfred Schutz, *Collected Papers,* Vols. I and II (The Hague, Martinus Nijhoff, 1962, 1964) and *The Phenomenology of the Social World,* translated by George Walsh and Frederick Lehnert (Evanston, Ill., Northwestern University Press, 1967), for a profound discussion of the character of the everyday world, especially its nondoubted quality.

Seeing Detroit in flames in July of 1967 was a shattering event for whites. All the old ways of thinking that told us Detroit was the most advanced city in race relations were blasted apart. Why have a catastrophe here? I and most people with whom I talked were experiencing during and after these events fundamental changes in our interpretation of the times. The analysis of these events differed from person to person and differed within the same people at different times. For some whites, what initially was termed a riot was later called rebellion. For others, what was first a riot became an additional step toward total anarchy.

We have seen already that the introduction of the concept of black power shattered white expectations. Blacks had never acted so violently. For most whites, black power represents racism at its worst. For others, it carries the hope of a better future for whites as well as for blacks.

Ours is a time particularly conducive to change, but we need to provide white Americans with a roadmap for the future. The roads on the old maps seem to be dead end. New whites will have to chart new courses.

CHAPTER II

ETHICAL CLARITY FOR NEW WHITES

I. QUESTIONS OF STANDARDS

Societal change is not good in itself. It is understood and evaluated by some set of standards. None of us escapes evaluating it. We read in a newspaper that a fourteen-year-old son sues his father, with whom he is living, for support. We react evaluatively. We see pictures of men burning themselves to death in protest over certain social conditions; we witness civil disturbances, in person or on television; and we react evaluatively.

Standards are an integral part of the orientation any of us uses to make sense of our situations. When shifting orientations, certain problems arise.

First, more effort than usual is required to clarify standards. With the old, set ways of thinking, standards are so deeply ingrained that they operate automatically. A person does not have to articulate his standards to decide whether he approves or disapproves of certain societal developments. However, when pressed to clarify those standards and relate them to each other, that same person is often forced to silence or incoherent rambling. It is a rare person who is lucid about his evaluative criteria. The criteria are present, but only implicitly.

Shifting from an old to a new orientation requires that implicit standards become explicit. We can no longer permit the old criteria to go unchallenged. If they do go unchallenged they may direct us along avenues dictated by the old orientation rather than suggest new ways. Even when challenged, the criteria may not necessarily be replaced. But at least they have been reevaluated and cast in a new context.

Any emerging new consciousness is constantly tested by its capacity to organize a plethora of data into fresh and meaningful patterns. This cannot occur without clarity of standards. If the data are too complex and orientation too uncertain, we will revert to older, more familiar ways of thinking. When one is traveling over unsure terrain, an old map is more comforting than no map at all. New white consciousness is remapping the terrain. We risk failure, frustration, and the lure and comfort of familiarity. Nevertheless, if we are to develop new white consciousness, we must know what we stand for and why.

Second, rationalization easily blurs disciplined analysis. Once we have begun the process of clarification of standards, we face another temptation — to disguise real reasons with spurious reasons. Our evaluative criteria are so much a part of us that when we feel one of them is under attack, we frequently send out smoke screens to blur what we really stand for. An effective smoke screen is a plausible appeal to standards. It becomes a quasi-standard — partly justifiable and partly a dodge from the real issues under question. Whites can give a long list of "reasons" for refusing to live with blacks. Are they justifiable reasons or rationalizations? In order to avoid perpetuation of subtle and unexamined rationalization, we need clarity in our standards.

Third, there is the problem of confusing sources of standards with reasons for their acceptance. If asked the source of our standards, we could give a long list — parents, church-synagogue, special friend, street gang, Bible, literature, American culture. However, the question of proper grounds for accepting or rejecting standards differs fundamentally from questions of source. Even if we admit that many of our standards (and there are many[1]) come from our parents, it does not follow that whatever our parents taught us should be accepted. We evaluate our sources by criteria other than the source itself.

This distinction is particularly important for a new white. He can draw on many sources in the past — conservative,

---

[1] See Robin Williams, *American Society* (N. Y., Knopf, 1966), especially ch. 11 on "Values and Beliefs in American Society," pp. 397ff.

liberal, right-wing, left-wing, religious, secular — without feeling that he is abdicating to a particular group. Most groups and ideologies express some dimension of truth. The new white should be clear enough in his own understanding of what he stands for and why, that he can see similarities and differences in groups and draw upon many seemingly conflicting sources.

And finally, there is a problem of parochialism in the grounding of standards. A new consciousness for whites cannot endure if in its efforts to justify its standards, it is limited to appeals to evidence or data not generally available to all whites. Appeals to religious revelation or particular personal experiences, for example, are critical to some people but unimportant and unavailable to others. New white consciousness, to be broadly received and understood, should be based on common human experience clarified by common reasoned inquiry. Any other approach excludes some groups right from the beginning.[2]

The task before us then is fourfold: (1) to clarify our standards and discern their interrelationship, (2) to fight rationalization, (3) to distinguish sources and reasons, and

---

[2] Recently there has been much discussion and confusion about the status of values and standards of justice. For many theologians, philosophers, and social scientists, the impact of the idea of cultural relativity has undercut the search for universal and necessary norms. See H. R. Niebuhr, *The Meaning of Revelation* (N. Y., Macmillan, 1960), especially pp. 7ff. Accompanying the argument about relativity and its implied attack upon any secure foundation for values was another argument—that values are a matter of commitment and perspective. In the final analysis different value perspectives are not debatable. This latter approach to normative discourse deterred efforts to search for and justify values through reasoned inquiry. Normative discourse depended on perspectives that were not negotiable; they were a nondoubted presupposition through which one interpreted life.

For an increasing number of social philosophers and theologians, these attacks on values and the criteria of justice were less victorious than the first skirmishes suggested. We cannot examine the reason for these shifts. It has become apparent to most, however, that one cannot move from descriptive relativism, which is almost universally accepted, to a view that suggests that there is no valid way of articulating and justifying one value or ethical principle against another. See William Frankena, *Ethics* (Englewood Cliffs, N. J., Prentice-Hall, 1963), esp. pp. 92ff.

(4) to build a model based on common experience and reasoned inquiry. In this chapter a model is developed along these lines.

II. ELEMENTS OF COMMUNICATION

Consciousness presupposes communication. We send signals, receive signals, and constantly interpret the signals we send and receive within some context of meaning. There is no such thing as a human being divorced from the web of human interaction. Even the hermit, the symbol of voluntary physical isolation, carries with him the marks of the human community. His language, his self-image, his feelings, are all results of social interaction. We all are in continual communication with whatever surrounds us. We cannot become human alone.

The pain of a friend's rebuke, the shared intimacy of a mother and daughter talking, the determination in the raised black fist, peace demonstrations, air pollution — all of these, plus millions more, contribute to the rich mix of human experience. As we mature, our consciousness changes and develops the orientations that help us comprehend the depths and heights of that experience. However, human development is neither always positive nor automatically guaranteed. Consciousness can become distorted. Behavior can be personally and socially destructive. Attitudes can become demonic.

If we can discern standards implicit in the very process of becoming human and justify these standards nonparochially, then we will be in a position to state with increasing confidence criteria for evaluating society's progress. To that task we now turn.

The most basic communication model involves three activities — gesture, response, and shared meaning. The slogan "black power" will illustrate how this model works.

(1) As a slogan it is first of all a *gesture* — a dynamic means of gaining attention; a signal demanding response. People were aware of the phrase "black power" long before they knew accurately what it meant.

Implicit in the act of initiating communication is *self-determination,* a recognition of one's own power and importance. Blacks who first talked of black power were aware

31

of the possibility and necessity of shaping their future. By initiating communication, a person necessarily affirms that he is self-determining.

(2) Gesture by itself is insufficient. Sending out a signal without appropriate *response* from the intended recipient is frustrating at best, as when talking to someone and suddenly realizing he is not listening. The gesturer wants response, but it must be the response of openness. Some structure, whether someone's mind or an institution, must be opened if the gesture is to be received.

Openness does not mean agreement. To be open is to take the gesturer with seriousness, but not necessarily to yield to his every point. It means to receive him as himself, without qualification.

Openness implies a second standard — *respect*. The gesturer wants the recipient to respect him as a person worthy of attention.

Respect is not the same as politeness. Politeness is usually a socially acceptable form of respect. Our children are taught frequently to equate politeness and respect. However, in serious conversation, politeness can be used to avoid honest encounter with people. People can be very polite in order to avoid being open to new data and fresh insight.

The gesturer expects the other person to be open and to respond to him as a person of worth. By this expectation the gesturer affirms his potential as a person with inherent dignity. He thus does not expect to be refused a hearing because of predetermined standards of behavior, status, or color. To respect is to be open and even to invite newness.

Those who were open to blacks and respected them were more likely to respond fairly to black power than those who regarded blacks as undeserving of attention and incapable of shaping their own programs for the future.

(3) The gesturer can send out a signal and the recipient can be open to receive it, yet communication can still be incomplete. There must be *shared meaning,* a common base of understanding that transforms the gesture into a significant and meaningful act.

Many whites construed black power in ways quite different from what was intended by the blacks who originated the slogan. (Yet, no one could miss one element of its message:

32

black people would no longer passively accept domination and abuse by whites.) Similarly, the response to the upraised, gloved fists of black participants in the 1968 Olympics brought diverse reaction. Blacks hailed the event and were encouraged and sustained by it. Many whites denounced it as immature and unpatriotic. Without shared meaning, the intended signal could not be understood. Thus, to communicate, both parties require a common frame of reference in order to understand the intended meanings of each other's gestures.

Shared meaning implies a third standard — *pluralism.* Pluralism points to the reality of interdependence in communication. High on the list of insults someone can unintentionally give is to say, "I know exactly how you feel," or, "I know exactly what you mean." If we think about that statement for a minute, we know it is not true. No one can know exactly anything about any of us because no two people are exactly the same. No one experiences life exactly as I do because no one stands where I stand with my personal history. Yet we can communicate. Pluralism recognizes that there is shared meaning but never total overlap in meaning.

Pluralism lifts up the necessary and creative tension between similarity and difference. It is marked by variety, authentic options, diverse centers of power, and self-direction. Michael Novak, theologian and social commentator, really is describing a pluralistic association when he describes genuine community, which "recognizes that no one set of social pressures is sufficient to inspire the full range of human possibilities."[3]

It is a mistake to think that pluralism means everyone doing as he pleases or that all issues are equally important. Pluralism is not a contemporary form of rugged individualism or a form of relationship without priorities. Rather, pluralism recognizes societal interdependence and ongoing relationships which require coordination and setting of priorities. The problem facing advocates of pluralism is that of creating the proper priorities and developing the appropriate ten-

---

[3] Michael Novak, *A Theology for Radical Politics* (N. Y., Herder and Herder, 1969), p. 40.

sions between similarity and difference. We must ask what societal values and norms are essential for the new age.

The upheavals presently occurring in American society can be interpreted as the creative struggle for pluralism. What had been accepted as essential is no longer agreed to by many people. Styles of behavior and dress, for example, which many Americans deeply believe ought to conform to certain common standards, are being openly challenged.

The melting pot, a long-standing image of American hope, is under attack. Many people, especially in ethnic groups, are beginning to see that everyone loses when there is conformity to one definition of an American — the white anglo-saxon Protestant definition. The Jews lose; the Poles lose; the Italians lose; and the blacks, who were not permitted even to "melt," lose most of all. The richness of cultural heritage is lost. Names get changed, other languages go unused, ancient rites fade in memory, family stories die untold. Pluralism affirms ethnic variety, a variety that enriches all groups and traditions.[4]

Black power is attacking the prevailing definition of what whites consider essential. Whites no longer have the luxury of insensitively ignoring blacks. They have been put on notice that what was possible for black-white relationships three years ago is not possible today. Blacks demand a voice in any new definition of what is essential for American society.

The communicator, then, necessarily affirms three standards for himself — that he be *self-determining,* that he be given *respect,* and that he participate in *pluralistic* associations.[5]

If the gesturer necessarily claims these standards for himself, what then does he owe others? What is his justice obligation — his human obligation? *To be just is to guarantee*

---

[4] See Michael Novak, "Politicizing the Lower-Middle," *Commonweal,* XC, 12 (June 6, 1969), for a discussion of some of the political implications of ethnic pluralism.

[5] To demonstrate the truth of this assertion is to encourage skeptics to deny it. Any attempt to deny the values requires communication of the denial. That involves gesturing, demanding response and requiring shared meaning. Since the values are implicit and necessary in the communicative process, the skeptic will necessarily affirm the values in his efforts to deny them.

for others the implicit values one necessarily claims for one-self in the communicative act.[6] Since all human beings are potentially participants in the communicative act, it follows that all human beings are similar in affirming self-determination, respect, and pluralism. To be just, we ought to guarantee self-determination, respect, and pluralism for everyone.[7]

A diagram of the basic communication model can be pictured as follows:

Pluralism
Association
Shared Meaning

/\
/ Justice \
/ guaranteed \
/   for all   \
/_____\

Gesture   Response
| |
Power   Openness
| |
Self-determination   Respect

Although a gesturer necessarily affirms the three standards of justice for himself, he can delude himself into thinking that he can deny justice to others and still get justice for himself. He can try; but what he fails to realize is that authentic communication is mutual and interdependent. It is two-way. Thus for there to be actual social justice for the gesturer, whether an individual or a group, he must guarantee it for all other parties as well.

There are three analytically distinguishable but inter-

---

[6] This ethical principle is a modification of one suggested by Alan Gewirth in an unpublished paper "Categorical Consistency in Ethics," delivered at the University of Chicago in 1966. The triatic communication model was developed from Gibson Winter's *Elements for a Social Ethic.*

[7] The justification for the ethical principle is based on the principle of noncontradiction. To justify treating similar people dissimilarly is self-contradictory. The negation of the principle affirms it.

related dimensions of being just or human. In any relationship, whether it be face to face, small group to small group, or major institution to major institution, there are power dimensions, structural dimensions, and normative dimensions.

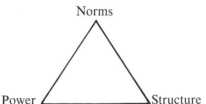

A gesturer seeks or demands response from some structure, be it a person or an institution, and legitimates that action by appealing to some norms that are at least partially shared. Any denial of justice in one dimension distorts the other two. Power, structure, and norms can each become dehumanizing and fail to support self-determination, respect, and pluralism in theory as well as in practice.

III. ELEMENTS OF NONCOMMUNICATION

Denial of the standards of just communication results in noncommunication. A look at the unjust expressions of the standards will help us to do two things: one, gain greater clarity about the meaning of self-determination, respect, and pluralism, and two, set the foundation to define racism in the next chapter.

The unjust expression of self-determination is *domination*. Domination is the arbitrary and one-way assertion of authority by one person, group, institution, or culture over another person, group, institution, or culture. An action is arbitrary when no justification for the action can be given other than the assertion of the authority itself. A child who asks why he has to wash his hands and is told by his father, "Because I said so," experiences arbitrary authority. Although the father may be responding in exasperation or because of expediency, he is saying in effect, "I can do as I please without giving any reasons." This kind of relationship is tragic enough in face-to-face relationships. It assumes cancerous proportions when groups and institutions operate on this principle.

However, groups and institutions seldom give "because I said so" as a reason for their arbitrary use of power. Spokesmen convincingly rationalize any action taken. One has only to think of all the "reasons" a company gives for having no black people in top management positions. While the rationalizations may go on and on, the effect is the same: an arbitrary decision is made first and the arguments to protect it are developed later.

Another element in domination is the one-way use of power, or elitism. Decision-making is reserved for a few rather than being widely distributed. We should be wary about any group that claims to be working for our welfare and yet overtly or covertly denies our participation in those decisions. There are many seductive forms of elitism. Some of the more dangerous are exhibited by those persons who speak most fervently about participation for all.[8] The culture can also dominate. It can perpetuate myths from the past that, even though untrue, shape people's perceptions of who and what are problems and what ought to be done about them. The culture can dominate when the myth is so pervasive that almost no gesture toward truth can dislodge it.

The result of domination is powerlessness. Individuals and groups cannot get attention, cannot be heard, and are denied some significant influence over their futures. Domination stifles gesturing. Under increasing domination, the gesturer is limited in his options to respond. Finally, the choice becomes one of three: give in totally, fight with whatever resources are available, or play-act, that is, perform one way publicly and another way privately.

The unjust expression of respect is *closure,* which cuts off potential in others. If in encounters we encase the other with rigid expectations and fail to receive new data from him, both of us are diminished and dehumanized. The same holds true for institutional arrangements. For example, roles can be so narrowly defined that a person is straitjacketed rather than liberated. Denial of respect also manifests itself institutionally when groups or individuals are denied access to social resources. Without good health, sound

---

[8] This analysis begs the question of how participation ought to be structured in society.

education, and political and economic power, men and women cannot function effectively in a complex technological society. Functional underdevelopment is the result of a closed society.

Cultural closure occurs when fresh insight is blocked by preconceived patterns and inherited traditions. For example, today many men and women are struggling to gain new understanding of what it means to be husband and wife. If the dominant norms for that relationship legitimate male domination and undercut female self-determination, then the culture is blocking an authentic expression of a new personal and institutional relationship. As such, it is unjust.

Finally, unjust expressions of pluralism are *alienation* and *assimilation*. Pluralism emphasizes similarity and difference in tension together. Alienation stresses difference; assimilation stresses similarity. The difficult task, as we have seen, is to maintain the proper tension, discerning what is absolutely essential for all, as distinct from what has only restricted significance. In such decisions, conflict is inevitable. Assimilation and alienation avoid conflict. Assimilation absorbs it, and tries prematurely to resolve or sidestep it through appeals to harmony and unity. Alienation excludes conflict by separating the conflicting parties and ignoring the real issues. In pluralistic associations conflict is expected and welcomed. It is interpreted as potentially creative; it is to be utilized.

Illustrations of the denial of pluralism are not difficult to find. Many a friendship and marriage has been destroyed because one partner tried to absorb the other into himself. Capitulation brought loss of self; resistance created alienation. Barring a pluralistic solution, estrangement, alienation, and separation were the only possible conclusions.

Groups frequently engage in similar patterns when they feel and believe that they have contrary goals and methods. Some revolutionaries, for example, claim there is "one best way" to bring about social change. Alternatives are rejected; assimilation is replaced by alienation.

Institutions develop deep-set patterns of assimilation. Since they stress relatively stable arrangements and practices, they press toward sameness. Recruitment practices, promotions, and most of the daily activities become established and are

38

difficult to change. As a result of the seeming permanence of structures, institutional leaders frequently confuse dissent and disloyalty. Structures become sacrosanct. When dissent occurs about those structures, it is easily misinterpreted. The gesture of protest is seen as a repudiation of some supposedly crucial practice. Instead of sorting out the strength and weakness of the argument, conflict is often avoided by an appeal to company loyalty. If that fails, then punitive action is frequently used. Punishment serves only to heighten alienation.

Cultural alienation and assimilation occur when the prevailing patterns and standards distort truth and suggest behavior appropriate to the myths. The myth of male superiority, or that blacks are the problem in race relations, are just two examples of cultural injustice. Because these myths are untrue but sustained in the culture, they undermine authentic pluralism and replace it with seemingly incomprehensible alienative or assimilationist interpretations of events.

The following chapter will show how denial of the necessary standards of communication is involved in racism.

CHAPTER III

NEW WHITES AND RACISM

The crucial task in gaining new white consciousness is to recognize our own racism. Many who use the term racism are hard pressed to define it. Often, when we at the Detroit Industrial Mission work with a white group on the problems of white racism, the group is broken into teams, each of which draws a picture of racism in their company. The only restriction is that no words may be used in the drawing. The artists, when asked specifically to identify the racism in their drawings, find it exceedingly difficult to do so. Racism sometimes means prejudice, sometimes discrimination, sometimes any concern with color; sometimes no response is given. Before we can proceed in this analysis, the term must be defined as it will be used here.

I. WHAT IS RACISM?

To be a full human being is to be self-determining, respected, and a participant in a pluralistic society. A just society maximizes these three standards of justice — self-determination, respect, and pluralism — for all. Racism de-

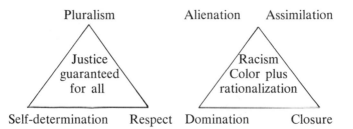

Pluralism / Justice guaranteed for all / Self-determination — Respect

Alienation — Assimilation / Racism Color plus rationalization / Domination — Closure

nies each. Racism is inherently unjust, totally unjustifiable, and humanly destructive. Basically, *racism is any activity by individuals, groups, institutions, or cultures that treats human beings unjustly because of color and rationalizes that treatment by attributing to them undesirable biological, psychological, social, or cultural characteristics.*

As a result of supposed racial differences, individuals or groups in one society claim superiority over other racial groups. The self-designated superior group, because of differences attributed to another bloc of persons, feels justified in violating the three standards of justice while simultaneously believing in its own virtue.

Who has ever heard a Northerner admit he did something because he was a racist? Our propensity for moral justification does not permit it. Rather, our racism is couched in quasi-moral terms which command social respectability and accrue social acceptance to us. Frank Joyce, founder of People Against Racism, spots some of these rationalizations:

> Schools are segregated not to keep blacks separate but to "preserve the neighborhood school." Police are given excessive power in the ghetto not to deny basic constitutional rights to second-class-citizen black people but to stop "crime in the streets." Blacks are not denied jobs because of their skin color but because they are not "qualified." Housing integration is not opposed because people do not wish to live next door to "niggers," but because black people lower property values. Black students, it is argued, fail to learn in ghetto schools not because the schools are inferior, but because the black students are inferior by virtue of "cultural disadvantagement" and of poor home environment.[1]

Because most whites deny that color is the reason for rejecting blacks, the phrase "attributed biological, psychological, social, or cultural characteristics" has been included in the definition of racism. Whites react on a "color-plus" basis — black plus laziness, black plus immorality, black plus militancy, etc. This color-plus response from whites makes it very difficult for whites to recognize and admit

---

[1] Frank Joyce, "Introduction, Definition and Analysis," unpublished paper of People Against Racism, p. 3.

their own racism. We can be seduced by rationalizations and miss the racist signal.

One of the most blatantly racist signals is the equation of race with some kind of ethically relevant biological difference. If it can be supported that the races are fundamentally different, then the claim to equality of respect is at least questionable. The facts do not support the argument. "Anthropologists agree," writes Thomas Pettigrew, social psychologist and expert on racial studies, "that there is only *one* human species, immodestly named *homo sapiens* ('wise man'). But there are many varieties of this one species."[2] Any effort to get rigid categories by which to divide the races biologically is always confronted with exceptions. There is either one race — mankind — or an indefinite number of races, depending on what criteria are selected.[3]

Efforts by whites to justify racism on biological grounds are factually without basis. They are usually attempts to undergird racist social and cultural commitments. Reporting the biological facts does little to change the white stance. Much more is at stake than simply biological considerations.

Many whites, accepting as truth a whole range of psychological, social and cultural plusses, see no racism in their beliefs or in what they are doing. Racism in America is so inherent that gaining sufficient distance from ourselves and society to recognize it is a difficult task.

This insensitivity to our racism only compounds its demonic nature. Racism is doubly destructive — it destroys the victims, who are treated as less than human; and it destroys the perpetrators, who perceive themselves as human. In America, the results of victimization are increasingly obvious. We are just beginning, however, to grasp the breadth and depth of the self-deception, hate, and long-term political and economic losses sustained by whites from racism. "White Americans," observes Frank Joyce, "do not know who they are because in 1607 and before, they have constructed an identity that depends primarily on who they are *not*. Because of this, they have brutalized not only men and women

---

[2] Thomas Pettigrew, *A Profile of the Negro American* (Princeton, N. J., Van Nostrand, 1964), p. 59.

[3] See the rest of ch. 3 in Pettigrew for further discussion on the concept of race, pp. 59ff.

of color, but, perhaps irrevocably, themselves as well."[4] This negative self-image has penetrated so deeply into white identity that most whites find it almost impossible to conceive of themselves as the root problem of racist America. Whites are preoccupied with fears of supposed black racism to the almost total avoidance of very real white racism. To them, blacks continue to be the problem, and they continue to be angry that the problem does not go away.

II. WHERE IS RACISM?

All of American society is infected with racism, but not everything that Americans do is racist. In order to avoid the trap of crying "wolf" at everything that occurs in American society, we need to be able to discriminate what are and what are not expressions of racism.

Most discussions of racism identify two places for its expression — institutions and individuals. This distinction is extremely important because it makes clear that well-intentioned people can perpetuate racism in institutions even though they themselves have never personally engaged in overt acts of racial injustice. As valuable as this distinction is, it ignores another crucial place for analysis — the cultural or belief system of the American that sets his orientation in the decision-making process.

Each of us, it was argued earlier, has some broad framework which permits us to make sense out of our experience. This framework carries forward the meaning and significance of what is happening. The attack on institutional and individual racism fails to show the extent of a racist mentality that legitimates and justifies institutional and individual acts of racism.

Belief systems or frameworks transcend any given institution. Thus, a businessman in Detroit and a businessman in Los Angeles may have very similar basic orientations to the racial and urban situation. To the victim of racism it may appear that these two men have conspired with each other to maintain white supremacy. However, what is more likely is that these two men have inherited a way of organizing and making sense out of the racial situation that is nearly

---

[4] Joyce, p. 2.

43

universal in America and leads to expression of the same views, even though they have never met each other.

In light of these remarks, this analysis will center around the three places of racism — culture, institutions, and individuals. Since much written material is already available on individual and institutional racism, the cultural aspect will be emphasized here.

A. CULTURAL RACISM

1. Historical Myths

Cultural racism is expressed in our historical myths that romanticize the past as Thanksgiving does, for example. Recently a number of whites were asked to list the meaning of Thanksgiving as it is celebrated in American society. The group talked about the Pilgrims' joy at having safely survived the first year, the gift of the new land to the Pilgrims, the help of the Indians, and celebrating the harvest. Asked to think specifically about the Thanksgiving feast in relation to the Indians, the group was quite clear that the Indians, in fact, made it possible for the whites to survive in the new land. Then they were asked to reflect on white America's relation with the Indians after that period of celebration. After some uneasiness, group members admitted that white settlers assumed that the land belonged to the whites and that Indians were expendable if they resisted the takeover. Thanksgiving, they came to realize, has been romanticized. In reality it represented the first step in a systematic white takeover from initially friendly and cooperative Indians.

The same group was asked to consider how our school textbooks write about the opening of the West. It became quite clear that from the white point of view, the opening of the West was justified by any means necessary. Treaties were made and broken regularly as whites felt they had a "manifest destiny" to secure the West from the "savages" and make it safe for white, civilized habitation. Today, whites have the audacity to talk about "Indian-givers" as if the Indians were the problem.

It is imperative that new whites become intimately conversant with their past, for one method of dealing with cultural racism is to destroy the myths that support it. Many whites, however, when confronted by the racism in American history, refuse to deal with it. The usual response is: "We aren't responsible for the past. We are not slaveowners. We didn't do all that. We want to start over. Forget the past and think about the future."

This response is quasi-moral, because it is only partially true. New beginnings are possible; change is possible. The call to forget the past is also a dodge, however. It is another refusal to accept the profound consequences of ourselves being the problem. Efforts to deny the results of the past do not make the results disappear. We cannot finally make sense out of racism independently of a full historical perspective.[5] Examination of the past is not done to intensify guilt. We do not need another "guilt-in." Historical examination emphasizes that the issues we are dealing with today have deep roots in the past and cannot be solved without recognizing consequences of earlier decisions.[6]

2. *Contemporary Language*

Not only is cultural racism widespread in the romanticized myths of the past; it is embodied in our everyday language. Language, we have learned from philosophers and social scientists, acts as a lens or filter that helps sort and evaluate our experience. Words are not neatly definable; they carry with them multiple meanings which shade off into each other. As such, some words have emotional content that is not always easy to specify. Two such words are white and black. Whiteness is celebrated as a good while blackness is castigated as bad.

To test this observation, try to think of derogatory uses of white. White lie? No, a white lie is an acceptable lie. In the same regard, try to think of good uses of black. When this exercise was tried with white groups, one session produced a single bad use of white — to whitewash an issue. But on reflection the group realized that even that use had a twist to it. To whitewash something is to make a bad situation acceptable — by making it white! The same group

---

[5] Although not quoted here, many of PAR's publications provide valuable historical analysis of American racism.

[6] See Douglass Fitch, "Doing My Thing," *Life and Work*, XI, 2 (1969), for an excellent thematic rendering of black and white history.

found two good uses of black — financial books in the black and black soil. The group admitted, however, that both examples were fuzzy. Financial black was contrasted with red, not white; black soil was descriptive, not metaphorical and analogical. The search for negative uses of black produced a long list. We blackball people, death is black, sin is black, a gloomy future looks black, a bad lie is a black lie. Positive uses of white produced a similar extensive list. To become pure is to become as white as snow. Angels are pictured as white. And a "white-hat special" is a good bargain.

When whites wonder why blacks make such a point over being called black — whether they are for it or against it — whites have only to reflect on how we use the white-black opposition. It is curious that, while many whites have no problem calling themselves white — which, literally, they are not — at the same time they often refuse to call blacks black. The reason often cited is that to use the term black focuses mistakenly on color. Color consciousness should be avoided, and besides, blacks aren't really black! Perhaps a deeper reason is that whites are afraid of equating blacks with symbols of evil, a connection they feel but refuse to admit openly.

3. *White Standards*

Cultural racism imposes white standards on other racial groups. Whiteness dominates. Recently, in a Detroit newspaper, an announcement was made that signs like the one pictured below were going to be installed at all school zones and crossings in Detroit.

Although the color of the sign was to be white on purple, it was clear that the children were white children. Cultural racism is white ethnocentrism. We do not doubt that white is right, and we impose this frame of reference on others without any sensitivity to their reactions.[7] When this example is presented to white groups, the reaction is mixed. While some people quickly see what is going on here, other whites immediately think of the opposite alternative. They say, "Well, what are we to do, put pictures of black children on all the signs, even in white communities?" They fail to do the imaginative thinking that could press artists to design pluralistic alternatives.

Only recently have the mass media, especially advertising, begun to counteract white cultural domination. The action is so recent that we continue to be surprised when a black man or woman appears in a TV ad. Even so, there is still a feeling that these advertisements are contrived. The proportion of black to white is carefully maintained and the roles meticulously defined. One cannot help wondering whose cultural criteria are being employed to decide appropriate style of dress, language, and roles for blacks.

4. Confrontation with Black Power

Perhaps the most dramatic place to see cultural racism in action is in the confrontation between liberals, conservatives, and black power advocates. White responses to black power were noted earlier, but now the orientations behind those white responses will be analyzed. As new whites, we need to know the dominant orientations that inform, direct, and make sense out of old white behavior.

a. Typical Critique of Black Power

The black power movement has been thoroughly criticized by liberal and conservative whites alike. The criticism can be grouped into three categories. Whites have argued that black power is fundamentally unjust; that it denies pluralism, respect, and self-determination.

(1) Black power denies pluralism. Black power is dividing the community. Instead of fostering communication and

---

[7] See The 'Rightness of Whiteness' by Abraham F. Citron, Michigan and Ohio Regional Educational Laboratories, February 1969.

unity, it polarizes the community by increasing hostility, suspicion, and violence. All the talk of creating two nations, a white and a black, is antithetical to an integrated society. Black power is separatist, racist, and divisive. It turns blacks against whites at a time when understanding and cooperation are desperately needed. Black power violates the principle of pluralism and fosters alienation rather than creative variety.

(2) Black power denies respect. Black power encourages a new racial superiority. Blacks are coming to feel that they are better than whites. They actually advocate reverse discrimination. Blacks think that they are above the law, a law that applies to blacks and whites alike. Black power encourages disrespect of all persons who disagree with a certain view of what it means to be black. Black power violates the principle of respect. It is actually closed to other groups.

(3) Black power denies self-determination. Black power encourages the domination of blacks over whites. Where in the past the whites have dominated the blacks, now it is time for blacks to take control. Blacks want arbitrary power and arbitrary control. Thus, black power is a movement to take over the power structure of the United States. Black power violates the principle of self-determination. It is encouraging the domination of one race over another.

These criticisms of black power express the demonic inversion of white racism. For the racist, pro-white necessarily means anti-black. Thus, for anyone to be pro-black, he must be anti-white. But to those especially who are familiar with black power the fallacy of such thinking is obvious.[8]

Conservatives and liberals both fall prey to this racist negation of black power. They are the old whites who operate with racist orientations and advocate racist solutions.

b. Conservative and Liberal Models

Old whites in America usually use one of two models to interpret current political and social events. These models are both descriptive and prescriptive. That is, they provide the user with meaningful guidelines to understand what is

---

[8] This essay is not on black power. For those readers interested in understanding the literature and claims of the movement, a suggested bibliography is included at the end of this volume.

happening and what ought to happen. These two models are labeled conservative and liberal, although most men so labeled resist such categorization. The terms will be used in this essay to identify major themes of each orientation. Obviously no one person totally fits either category. However, there is enough difference in orientation to justify the distinction.

(1) Conservative Model — Distribution of Power

> State power, considered in the abstract, need not restrict freedom; but absolute state power always does. The *legitimate* functions of government are actually conducive to freedom. Maintaining internal order, keeping foreign foes at bay, administering justice, removing obstacles to the free interchange of goods — the exercise of these powers makes it possible for men to follow their chosen pursuits with maximum freedom. But note that the very instrument by which these desirable ends are achieved *can* be the instrument for achieving undesirable ends — that government can, instead of extending freedom, restrict freedom. And note, secondly, that "can" quickly becomes "will" the moment the holders of governmental power are left to their own devices. This is because of the corrupting influence of power, the natural tendency of men who possess *some* power to take unto themselves *more* power. The tendency leads eventually to the acquisition of *all* power — whether in the hands of one or many makes little difference to the freedom of those left on the outside.[9]

When asked to identify the author of this quote, white groups have named Jefferson, Washington, Thoreau, Eldridge Cleaver, Stokely Carmichael, Alexander Hamilton, and other political figures. In fact, the statement appeared in *The Conscience of a Conservative,* a book in which Barry Goldwater argues forcefully for a particular way to understand power and government.

Conservatives are clear advocates of limited government and maximum self-determination for all people. Every man, they argue, has the right to be a spontaneous, vital, self-

---

[9] Barry Goldwater, *Conscience of a Conservative* (Shepherdsville, Ky., Victor Publishing Co., 1960), p. 17. In this section, we point to only one contradiction between thought and practice. There are certainly others, e.g., the support of business interest at the expense of the consumer.

initiating center of creativity and action. The proper role for government is to permit self-determination of each man while guaranteeing self-determination for all men. Power in this view is the pursuit of private interests and harmony with other people's pursuit of their private interests. Government, at its best, serves a regulatory and coordinating function. Its goal is to maintain an open, pluralistic society.

There is in this view a deep suspicion of any centralization of power, of any control of one group by another group. The solution to concentration of power is distribution of power through competition and local control. Inherent in this view is the responsibility of each person for the shape of his future. Responsibility focuses on individual initiative and individual accountability. To be responsible is to stand with integrity against the encroachment of government and to stand for self-determination for all men.

(2) Liberal Model — Societal Health. In an in-depth interview, one of America's leading liberal spokesmen set before us some of his deepest convictions about self and society.

Q: First, about two of the major questions — of peace at home and abroad — why, at this moment in history, do we find such incredible conflagrations — those in the universities; the civil rights battle; the problems abroad; so many things relating to violence?

A: ... I do not look with fear and foreboding upon what is happening. I think that it is essentially a process of the growth of freedom. . . . Really he [Adlai Stevenson] was saying that this process of growth and freedom takes time, just as maturation does with an individual.

Later in the interview he was asked:

Q: Do you feel, from your knowledge of the American people, that we're ready for that kind of total social planning?

A: I think that we're not only ready for it; I think that readiness depends on necessity. The necessity of it is going to compel it . . . we do what works. And we try — trial and error — and we're just beginning to find out that it's just plain bad economics and bad business and bad government to have riots and violence and the poor that are deprived. . . . We found, for example, in Project Head Start something that we ought to

50

have known a long time ago, that if you get to a child
soon enough with proper diet, proper care, reasonably
good environment, with modern teaching methods, he
just blossoms.... It's like what I've seen at home...
in the drought. One good rain, and the corn grew
three inches....[10]

The spokesman, Hubert Humphrey, presents a liberal
definition of self and society which is different from that of
the conservative. Conservatives stress the spontaneous creative capacity of man; and they fear dominant powerful and
all-encompassing organizations, especially government. Liberals, in contrast, propose an organic view of man and society. Conservatives tend to set man in tension with government and focus on distribution of power as the key issue.
Liberals picture man as a part of a developing society and
focus on the healthy growth of "man in society" as the key
issue. Liberals stress socialization, therapy, education, economic aid, and other massive institutional programs to encourage societal growth. It is not accidental that Humphrey
used agricultural and health metaphors in his interview. Liberals are deeply committed to the proposition that proper
family life, healthy personalities, sound education, and economic assistance are essential to societal growth and development. Without them there is no possibility of self-determination, respect, and pluralism.

The concentration of power in government is less feared
by liberals than by conservatives. This is due in large measure to differing definitions of the nature of man and society.
For the conservative, concentrations of power necessarily
threaten a spontaneous dynamic self, since that power must
limit spontaneous activity. A person should be able to do
as he pleases as long as he does not violate the same right
for others.

The liberal, on the other hand, does not view the self as a
spontaneous center. Instead, the self is more like a seed,
which when properly watered will grow and bloom. Good
power operates through institutional programs to make
"blooming" possible. Power, then, could be centralized in

10 "This Process of Growth and Freedom, an Interview with Hubert H. Humphrey," by Richard Heffner, *Saturday Review* (October
12, 1968), pp. 22-24.

government if that power provided growth programs for the whole population. Responsibility demands obedience for the development of the whole social fabric.

So far we have explored two models that provide liberals and conservatives with basic orientations to understand what is and ought to happen in society. The racism appears in these two stances when they confront black power.

c. Conservative Racism

The conservative is the great advocate of self-determination and local control.[11] Yet, when confronted with black power's demand for self-determination and local control, the conservative usually chooses domination, government control, and the maintenance of white power. The conservative does not believe he is racially motivated. His racism is disguised by the quasi-moral issue of law and order. By appealing to that issue, a conservative can "morally" maintain his racism, justify his opposition to black power, and simultaneously support stronger crime legislation, including stop-and-frisk laws and greater police armaments. Paradoxically, advocates of limited power for government are so threatened by black power that they are willing to contradict their own deepest convictions to maintain white power. They strengthen the institutions they supposedly fear the most — government and the police.

Racism, with the fears, anxieties, and myths it perpetuates, divides conservatives and black power advocates. White conservatives are under the illusion that they are working to save the nation from anarchists, revolutionaries, communists, and others seeking to destroy the country. Thus, for "moral" reasons they support efforts to maintain law and order by increasing military, police, and governmental control. The tragic irony is that the conservative's action may well be contributing to the destruction of the country. Racism has so blinded white conservatives that their own deepest insight into man and government, which could be a creative contribution to American society, has become one of the most demonic. In the conservative's racist orientation, blacks are the problem — especially militant blacks — and they

---

[11] The conservative's basic model of power is closest to the position taken by Stokely Carmichael and Charles Hamilton in *Black Power*.

must be stopped by whatever means are necessary and punished for their activity. What the conservative does not understand is that law and order can be maintained only when there is equitable distribution of power. It is the white who is the greatest violator of law and order. The conservative's deepest insight on self-determination is sound, but his racism destroys the potential for that insight to be created into authentic justice for blacks and whites alike.

d. Liberal Racism

The liberal is the advocate of healthy societal growth.[12] He appears to understand, more than the conservative, the decisive importance of institutions on man's development in the world. Furthermore, he had been, he thought, the white advocate of the black cause. The liberal was deeply moved to help cure what he perceived as the sicknesses running almost unchecked in poor black ghettos. Political liberals worked legislatively to create massive institutional programs to rid America of its sickness and restore health to the whole community.

The confrontation with black power has been disastrous for the liberal. The white liberal is denounced as more dangerously racist than the conservative. What is behind this denunciation?

The implicit assumption of white liberals is that white-dominated and white-controlled institutions and culture are healthy while black counterparts are sick. The liberal, from his self-designated stance of health, is justified then in setting up programs to cure the black from his sickness.

Black power exposes this racist myth. Black power calls for white Americans to realize that the deepest sickness lies with the white community, not the black. America's race problem is a white problem, not a black problem. Black power, with its deep commitments to self-determination, respect, and pluralism, is a bearer of a new humanity. The white liberal is not a source of new humanity, but the perpetuator of white sickness. From a black point of view,

---

[12] The liberal's basic model of societal health is closest to that of Nathan Wright in *Black Power and Urban Unrest* and "The Ethics of Power and the Black Revolution," a presentation to the American Society of Christian Ethics, January 26, 1969.

the self-appointed saviors of America are its greatest de-
tractors. They blur the real issues. Through liberal "concern for the Negro" the basic problem of pervasive white
racism is sidestepped.

Because the liberal feels he has been maligned by blacks
and radical whites alike, perhaps we should take some space
to explore the liberal plight. The white liberal has consistently argued for open structures and from time to time ad-
vocated pluralism. However, he has set standards that created closure and thus enhanced assimilation or alienation.
The liberal pushed programs to let blacks into the mainstream of American life but all too often personally separated himself from the integrated society he was recom-
mending. This ambiguity is captured by Louis Lomax, author
and social commentator, in his astute description of a
white liberal:

> The white liberal is not a happy man. . . . He is the Jew
> admitting that he is no longer a chosen man but silently
> wondering why Negroes don't stick together and help each
> other and live together like the Jews do; he is the Catholic
> appalled by the fact that he has so long prayed that God
> would forgive the perfidious Jews but unable to forsake
> a faith whose every trapping suggests that there is some-
> thing wrong with all non-Catholics; he is the white Anglo-
> Saxon Protestant marching along on the road from Selma
> while his eyes dart furtively toward the rising Negro crime
> rate; he is the clergyman torn between the new gospel he
> must now preach and the conservatism of the flock he
> must feed and which feeds him as well; he is the business-
> man quite willing to accept change so long as things re-
> main the same; he is the parent welcoming the new Negro
> neighbor and praying God that his daughter will marry
> one of her own kind . . . ; he is the child of the psychia-
> trist's couch, a man of conflicts, not contradictions; an
> advocate of change but an arch foe of revolution.[13]

These conflicts of the white liberal supported by this nation's massive, double-standard institutionalized structures
have almost destroyed the black community. In many ways

---

[13] Louis Lomax, "The White Liberal," in *The White Problem in
America,* Editors of Ebony (Chicago, Johnson Publishing Co., 1966),
pp. 41-42.

they have almost destroyed the white liberal community as well.

Of late, however, a new consistency is appearing among white liberals. Many of them have begun to recognize their racist double standard and are trying to overcome it. Alienation is now the target. *No man* in America should be estranged from the mainstream of American life. White institutions should be open. Out of the shift in orientation come many of the well-known social programs — the war on poverty, hard-core employment, and open housing. These programs are designed to provide the resources for alienated men to participate in white-dominated social, political, and economic structures. The program design was mostly by whites; the target for the program was mostly black.

As positive as some of these programs have sounded, they have (unintentionally in many cases) perpetuated an even more serious racist presupposition. Efforts to overcome alienation by assimilating blacks into the mainstream of American life have presupposed the mainstream as the desirable standard. Equality with whites is the goal. What the liberal does not understand is that equality with whites is a racist goal. Why should blacks want to be equal to white racists? It is actually a press for sameness. What it means for blacks is that they should enter the mainstream of a polluted river. Equality with whites is an assimilationist goal. What superficially appears as openness and respect is actually closure at a deeper dimension.

A good case in point is integration. Integration has been the key word in the liberal's racial vocabulary. It is the central organizing principle of the Kerner Report. Black separatism is just as much an enemy as white separatism to the liberal. Both challenge integration and both, he believes, are equally racist. Yet integration has received much scorn from supporters of black power, for at least two reasons.

First, black separatism is equated with white segregation. That is a racist mistake. The real separatists in the United States are whites. Integration did not fail because blacks did not want it; whites refused it. Thus the Kerner Report is in error when it concludes, "Our nation is moving toward two societies, one black, one white — separate and unequal." That presupposes that at one time there was one society.

Blacks clearly recognize that this was never true. Whites have continually maintained a separate, unequal, and closed society. Now whites are beginning to recognize this, and some are even worried about it. Black separatism simply recognizes a fact. The white community created the fact.

Second, integration is the liberal's "moral" phrasing of assimilation. The unity of black and white in white-dominated communities carries the expectation that blacks will conform to mores and norms of the white community, including styles of dress, care of property, and patterns of social life. Most whites would have little trouble living next door to a white Mafia leader. We know that most of the Mafia leadership live in the suburbs. They meet the overt community expectations. On the other hand many *new* whites find it increasingly difficult to live in suburban all-white communities. Integration tends, in fact, to stress the unimportant as important and leave to personal taste what a new white feels is crucially important.

The mobilization in some white communities for open occupancy legislation is sometimes cited as antiracist activity. However, as necessary as open occupancy is, the fact of open occupancy legislation as evidence of white good will can be the manifestation of a deeper racism. We expect blacks to move into our good neighborhoods. We hardly ever think of integrating in reverse — of our moving into predominantly black neighborhoods. When the idea of whites "integrating" black communities is suggested, a typical response is, "They might not want us. What would happen to our children in school? Their neighborhoods are not as good as ours." Yet, we spend little time thinking about the anxieties and fears of blacks moving into an all-white community or whether or not all-white neighborhoods are really that good. Whites allow blacks to risk the trauma of confronting whiteness, but dread the trauma of facing blackness.

The deeper issue in housing, however, is not whether blacks and whites live side by side but on what terms they live together. Blacks moving into white areas or the reverse can be equally closed and thus assimilationist. An alternative would be an experiment with a truly pluralistic community, where new blacks and new whites openly faced the issues of color and creative variety.

Black power is challenging an increasing number of whites to raise the question: Is white society so healthy that blacks should be integrated into it? The white liberal's unexamined presupposition of white healthiness is on shaky ground.

As with conservatives, the black confrontation exposes the liberal's willingness to negate his deepest insight. The liberals, the great advocates of health, are perpetuating programs that may sicken the whole society. They are paternalistically increasing the number of white-dominated government programs for "needy" blacks. Rather than recognize the new needs of black health and agree to massive transfers of political and economic power to the black community, the liberal continues and intensifies old programs like welfare and education. There might be some program updating. However, penetrating examination of existing programs is all too often missing. Because of the assumption that white institutions are not the fundamental problem, they do not get the critical attention they desperately need.

The liberal perpetuates racist programs not because he is a racist. He has a quasi-moral issue to blur the depths of his racism. Blacks are sick; whites are healthy. This guise takes on many forms. In each, however, white standards dominate. A well-intentioned liberal, asked why more blacks do not hold positions of decision-making power, quickly replies, "There aren't enough qualified men for the jobs." As with the law-and-order disguise, there is enough to the claim to make it plausible, but not enough to make it truthful. The cry of not enough qualified people often conceals the racist belief that blacks do not measure up to white criteria of acceptability.

An example of this problem was seen recently in a Chrysler manufacturing plant. Black demands for an increasing number of black foremen brought no response. The reply was that there were not enough qualified men to do the job. However, when an order from top management of the company was sent down, suddenly a number of black foremen were discovered. The quasi-moral issue is often a way of avoiding the transfer of power and responsibility. The argument implies that as long as there are no qualified blacks, whites must do the necessary jobs. Whites remain in charge. By appealing to this evasive device, the standards for admittance are not critiqued nor are new avenues of recruitment aggressively opened. However, it has been my experience that exploring multiple sources for recruitment of blacks uncovers many men who, under racist policies, have been unable to gain proper recognition for their talents. The post office, for example, is filled with many college graduates who could only find employment through a civil service or government route. Furthermore, when the standards are closely examined, some of what once was considered essential to the company often is seen to be in reality nonessential.

Of late I have encountered two different expressions of liberal concern for black qualifications. The first is exemplified in the speed by which many more radical, liberal whites have adopted the Negro-black distinction. What was originally a black man's categorization within his own community has become an evaluative distinction for many whites. All too frequently, one hears discussions in which whites are deciding if so-and-so is "black" or "Negro." "Negroes," of course, are middle-class sell-outs; "blacks" are the good confronters.

The racism becomes obvious. The same whites who had been advocates of black integration into middle-class society and who had set standards of acceptableness, now turn around, cast that group out, and support another group. Some whites, thinking themselves radical, want to hire only "blacks," not "Negroes." Whites continue to set the standards of acceptability; now "Negroes" are out and "blacks" are in. White selectivity remains.

A second illustration of white standard-setting was provided recently in Chicago. The Ecumenical Institute, committed to the changing of institutional structures, is located in the all-black west side of Chicago. The Institute is almost totally white. One of its projects has been named Fifth City. Fifth City is the geographical area surrounding the Institute. The goal is to enable indigenous black leadership to emerge and direct the future of that community. In discussions with a number of Institute staff members about the project, I asked them why they continued to remain in the black community, since whites, I maintained, should be working in the white community on the problems of white racism. After we had discussed that question, I asked what would make them leave Fifth City. They gave two answers. First, they would leave if they were thrown out by the black community. Second, they would leave when they felt the blacks were ready to assume responsibility for their own community. Both of these answers are racist. To expect the black community physically to throw out whites is to say that blacks have to take the responsibility and threat of legal punishment to attack a white establishment. The real losers in the confrontation would be the blacks, who would have to contend with a white-dominated police force and court system. The whites could simply leave and escape punishment. The contention that the Institute would leave when blacks had become qualified means that whites have set the standards of acceptability and expect the blacks to conform to them. The Institute expects blacks to accept a particular ideology and methodology for dealing with social change. The liberal pattern is evident even though disguised with revolutionary rhetoric. Standards are set to measure black response.

The liberal tragedy is that good intentions are blurred by implicit racism. The result is the liberal's inability to support healthy movements in society. In his view, blacks cannot be healthy; they are the problem. The liberal sees himself as necessary for blacks to become healthy.

e. New White Alternative

Both the conservative and the liberal misplace the problem in their orientations. As a result, they recommend solutions that are misguided and misplaced. The white conservative sees black disregard for law and order as the problem; his response is domination. The white liberal perceives the problem as black sickness; his response is closure. The conservative tends toward punishment. The liberal tends toward paternalism.

The new white inherits the old white legacy. Part of the conservative model, especially its emphasis on self-determination, can be affirmed. Part of the liberal model, especially its concern for societal health and institutional openness, can be affirmed. New whites, then, are in a position to work with both conservatives and liberals. Neither is a total enemy. Every old white is a potential new white.

What then is a new white alternative? If what I have argued is sound, the problem addressed by conservatives and liberals misses the larger issue of norms. The conservative stresses power; the liberal focuses on structure. Both refer to standards but neither grasps the error rooted in them. Because the conservative misdefines the problem, he supports policies and behavior that alienate black from white. Because the liberal misdefines the problem, he supports policies and behavior that assimilate black into white.

New white consciousness suggests that the underlying problem is the culture, the carrier of norms and standards, that sets the context of meaning through which we interpret our experiences. If American culture is racist, then reorganizing power and changing structures is necessary but not sufficient. The task for the new white is the long, hard, critical examination of the denials of pluralism in America. Once that analysis is opened, then new possibilities arise for restructuring power and institutions.

In order to accomplish this task a fundamentally different relationship between black and white must be developed. We have seen how punishment and paternalism both embody a culturally racist assumption. What alternative is there?

Occasionally, whites and blacks can develop very deep personal relationships of mutual trust. However, with the deepening awareness by blacks of what the real problem is in race, this possibility for personal relationships is decreasing. Blacks are correctly aware that old white consciousness, whether liberal or conservative, is not to black or, if properly understood, to white self-interest. Another base for relationship is needed.

In Detroit, some of us are exploring an alternative — *collaboration*. Collaboration is a relationship of peers committed to solving a common problem within a common framework. When both blacks and whites agree that the race problem is rooted in white racism, then there is the possibility for some joint strategy and tactic sessions. Both groups can agree that three dimensions of American experience must be changed — power, structure, and norms. Within that context, blacks strategize to eliminate white racism as experienced by the victims, new whites strategize to eliminate racism as expressed by the perpetrators.

Collaboration does not necessarily mean that blacks and whites continually confer with each other. They may only periodically check objectives, strategy, and tactics. Nor does it mean that whites must wait before they take action until any action is cleared with blacks. These kinds of decisions are contextual and depend almost totally on what objectives, strategies, and tactics are being planned and who is needed to carry them out.

One of the problems in developing collaborative black/white relationships is the lack of experience in this new kind of encounter. Old white ground rules, which we thought worked, no longer apply. New ground rules are only slowly emerging. At this stage we operate largely by trial and error. This method is nevertheless giving us clues on how to proceed, and a discussion of them can be found in Chapter VI.

The conservative, liberal, and new white positions can be summarized in the following chart:

Basic Orientation	Main Professed Value	Who Is the Problem?	Why?	Value Acted Out	Relation with Blacks
White conservative	Self-determination	Black power groups	Breakdown of law and order	Domination	Punishment
White liberal	Respect	Black institutions	Societal sickness	Closure	Paternalism
New white	Pluralism	White culture	Cultural white racism	Pluralism	Collaboration

B. INSTITUTIONAL RACISM

An excellent primer on institutional racism defines a racist institution:

> Institutions are fairly stable social arrangements and practices through which collective actions are taken. . . . Business and labor, for example, determine what is to be produced, how it is to be produced, and by whom and on whose behalf products will be created.

61

Institutions have great power to reward and penalize. They reward by providing career opportunities for some people and foreclosing them for others. They reward as well by the way social goods are distributed: by who receives training and skills, medical care, formal education, political influence, moral support and self-respect, productive employment, fair treatment by the law, decent housing, self-confidence and the promise of a secure future for self and children. No society will distribute social benefits in a perfectly equitable way. But no society need use race as a criteria to determine who will be rewarded and who punished. *Any nation which permits race to affect those who benefit from social policies is racist.*[14]

The Kerner Report concurs that American institutions are racist. It thoroughly documents institutional racism as the essential ingredient in American racist practice.

Institutional racism can be overt or covert, intentional or unintentional. Until World War II overt, intentional racism was practiced in the United States. The obvious patterns in the South and semi-disguised patterns in the North do not need repeating here. Since World War II, passage of various forms of civil rights legislation and official changes in government policy have withdrawn legal backing from overt, intentional, institutional racism. Lack of legality, of course, does not automatically eliminate racism. In the case of intentional racism, it just makes the overt more covert.

Mixed as it has been, the attack on overt, intentional, institutional racism has done little to attack covert and unintended institutional racism. In the primer on institutional racism, the authors argue that racism

is perpetuated nonetheless, sometimes by good citizens merely carrying on "business as usual," and sometimes by well-intentioned but naive reformers. . . . To detect institutional racism, especially when it is not intended and when it is disguised, is a very difficult task, and even when institutional racism is detected, it is seldom clear who is at fault. How can we say who is responsible for residential segregation, for poor education in ghetto schools, for extraordinarily high unemployment among black men,

---

[14] *Institutional Racism in American Society: A Primer,* Mid-Peninsula Ministry, April 15, 1968, pp. 2-3. Emphasis added.

for racial stereotypes in history text books, for the concentration of political power in white society?[15]

The task for new whites is to identify and fight against unintended and intended, covert and overt racism built into institutional structures that dominate American society.

There are many places to look for institutional racism. An article titled "Black Powerlessness in Chicago"[16] presents some dramatic data to demonstrate the extent of black exclusion from decision-making power. The essay reports that:

> In 1965 some 20% of the people in Cook County were Negro, and 28% of the people in Chicago were Negro. Yet the representation of Negroes in policy-making positions was minimal. Of the top 10,997 policy-making positions in major Cook County institutions included in our study, Negroes occupy only 285 or 2.6%.[17]

The study also states,

> The legal profession, represented by corporate law firms, had no Negroes at high policy levels. . . . The very prestigious universities — the University of Chicago, Northwestern University, Loyola University, DePaul University, Roosevelt University, the Illinois Institute of Technology, and the University of Illinois (the only public university of the seven) — had a negligible 1% Negro representation. Most of these universities have few Negro students, faculty members, or administrators. Five of the seven had no Negro policy makers.[18]

Even in major areas where Negro representation was greatest — labor unions — the statistics were not encouraging. The study continues,

> There are few Negroes in the building trades union, most of which bar Negroes from membership. Only two out of the twelve building trade union organizations we studied had even one Negro in the decisive slot. These two Negroes made up a mere 1% of the policy-making positions in the building trades unions. The greatest degree of black representation was found in the former CIO indus-

---

[15] *Ibid.*, pp. 3-4.
[16] Harold Baron, "Black Powerlessness in Chicago," *Trans-Action* (November 1968), pp. 27-33.
[17] *Ibid.*, p. 28.
[18] *Ibid.*, pp. 28-29.

trial unions. Only one-fourth of these unions in the survey totally excluded Negroes from leadership. In almost half, the percentage of Negro policy makers was over 15% — which is above token level.[19]

Finally, the study points out,

> In elective offices, the Negro vote certainly does give Negroes some representation — but far below their proportionate number. In public administration, however, where advancement to policy-making offices comes through appointment and influence, Negroes are all but excluded from decisive posts, at both the federal and local level. Although a very high percentage of all Negro professionals are in public service, they do not reach the top. The only major governmental operation that had a goodly number of Negroes at the upper level of the bureaucratic hierarchy was the public-school system. Nine per cent of the top positions were occupied by Negroes. This unique situation is the result of some fairly recent appointments, made as concessions after an intensive rights campaign directed at the Chicago Board of Education.[20]

Sadly, many whites who read studies of this type agree with the accuracy of the "facts" but do not see any institutional racism. Their orientation still tells them that blacks are the problem. White-dominated institutions cannot be at fault, they feel; it must be the lack of black initiative and qualifications.

Because of the difficulty men find in shifting their orientation from black to white, Dr. Alvin Pitcher and his associates on Chicago's Committee for One Society have developed a check list to help whites identify institutional racism. What follows is a listing of a few of the questions one can ask if possible locations of racism in a given company are to be isolated. A complete copy of the inventory can be found at the end of this book in the Appendix.

Employment: What percentage of workers are black? White? Male? Female? At each job level? How are employees recruited? Does the company have stated policies regarding equal employment opportunity? What are they? Is promotion a possibility for all employees? Is promotion a formal

---

[19] *Ibid.,* p. 30.
[20] *Ibid.*

process or is it the result of social contacts? Who ride together to work? Who eat lunch together? Do employees belong to social clubs? Outside of the company, what company business gets done? What types of jobs are people trained for? Are jobs marginal or subject to elimination by automation? What are employment benefits? Do all workers receive them? Is it policy to acquaint all employees with health insurance programs, for example? Do executives get stock options? Social club memberships? Is entry possible at all levels or must everyone come up through the ranks?

Services: Are black suppliers and services used? Scavengers? Exterminators? Janitorial services? Banking? Maintenance supplies?

Investments: What property is owned? Is property rented? What are the policies of the companies in which investments are made — in areas under consideration? Employment? Use of black services?

Advertising: What company is employed? Kind of contract? Size of account? Models employed? Images projected? Are black images projected in black media or in all media?

New Structures: Is there a company committee to develop and carry out a program for implementation of a nonracist policy? (A) Company officers appointed to supervise a program? (B) Regular examinations of compliance with policies? (C) Education of all levels of management? (D) Persons appointed to relate especially to black services and suppliers?[21]

Space does not permit illustrations of all the kinds of racism one might find if the inventory were taken seriously and applied to a given company. That task awaits doing by sensitive new whites in their own particular industrial location.

C. INDIVIDUAL RACISM

Most whites, if they are willing to use the word racism at all, think in terms of individual behavioral racism. They think of someone burning a cross on someone's lawn, throwing garbage on someone's grass, or calling a black man "nigger." Too many whites, who have never performed overt inten-

---

[21] Alvin Pitcher and Susan Tobias, *Inventory of Racism,* Committee for One Society, October 1, 1968, pp. 1-3.

tional acts of this type, feel able to exonerate themselves. If called racist they resent it deeply. It is for this reason that the categories of cultural and institutional racism are so crucial. None of us escapes being racist in American society. All of us participate in racist thought forms as well as institutional practices.

Examples of individual racism could fill volumes. Three are selected here from meetings of automobile company managers to illustrate unintentional and intentional racist behavior. One white man, trying to understand a distinction that was being made by a black man between Negro and black, asked the black man, "What do you mean by 'Negra'?" The black man immediately responded to this mispronunciation of Negro. It took three or four exchanges in the conversation before the white man realized that the pronunciation he had given was demeaning.

Another white man, after the meeting, went over to two young black resource men to thank them for sharing in the discussion. With the best intentions he said, "I just wanted to thank you boys for. . . ." He could not understand why the black men wouldn't shake hands with him.

At the same meeting a white man, after making a series of hostile and defensive remarks, finally said that he had only one other question he wanted to ask. He wanted to know why the black resource men kept their hats on at the meeting. It was more important to him to disparage blacks than to recognize his own unwillingness to accept hats as part of their uniform and communal identity. He clearly sought to denounce blacks by appealing to a standard that he thought most other men would accept. As it turned out, most of the men in the room felt his effort to put down the blacks was an expression of individual, intentional racism.

These are three brief examples of multiple ways in which whites express their racism. New whites will quickly develop their own lists and an astute sense of when racism is being expressed.

D. A TEST CASE

One way to test whether the racism analysis presented so far sharpens our capacity to locate and understand racist activity is to try it out on a case.

66

The Warner and Swazey Company of Cleveland placed the following advertisement in a popular business magazine:

THE *AMERICAN* WAY TO BLACK POWER

We know a company which doesn't give a snap for a man's color but only for his willingness to learn and work. Today there are more than 430 colored men and women there (15% of all employees), many of them among the supervisors, professionals, technicians and highest paid mechanics.

We know a lot about that company. It is Warner and Swazey, in its Cleveland plants.

Many of these people have been here for many years. They came here, not demanding anything but looking for a chance. They were glad to take *any* job, and some began as sweepers. We seriously consider and hire if we can (and we usually can) anyone who is neat, respectable, ambitious, with basic education — and we pay taxes in every one of our plant cities to *provide* that education *free*. We are in business to make a good product which people will buy, so that we can earn enough profit to pay those taxes and still keep on enlarging the business. We want workers regardless of color who will help us do it — workers who are *equal* to an *opportunity,* and who help create their *own* opportunity by productive work. And we believe the vast majority of American companies have exactly the same attitude.

Is this ad racist? If so, in what ways? Does it exhibit cultural, institutional, and/or individual racism? If so, how and in what way? What standards are used to judge a good worker? How do they match the standards of justice suggested earlier? What would a good antiracist ad look like on the same topic?

Racism is the absolute enemy of the new white. It is totally unjustifiable and totally unjust. The tasks are clear. Expose the contradictions, rationalizations, and disguises whites use to perpetuate racism. Face the multiple ways in in which all of us are victimized by racism. Challenge verbal commitments to justice and demand just action rather than mere talk. Finally, develop strategy and tactics appropriate to eliminating racism.

CHAPTER IV

SOCIAL STRATEGIES FOR CHANGE

Arthur Waskow, resident fellow at the Institute for Policy Studies in Washington, D.C., proposes a method of social change which provides the framework for this chapter. Introducing an article, he wrote:

> This paper will argue that one of the major tasks of liberal and radical thought in America today is to imagine the future in order that the future may be created. Briefly, my argument is that one of the most powerful ways of achieving social change is to imagine in vivid detail a desirable and achievable future, and then build a part of that future in the present.[1]

Intensely aware of the past, a major task of new whites is the construction of the future. Racism is the heritage; the future must be more than antiracist. The future is crucial for both the new white and the black, for America will either be transformed into a more authentic expression of justice or be destroyed.

Imagining and building a desirable and achievable future can occur at many levels. It can include various interests. For example, a man at Ford or Chrysler in middle management can imagine a future for his arena of power. Necessarily that will be smaller in scope than a vice president in the same company. But the extent of power does not negate the necessity for mapping a future and bringing it into being. Power not tested is power not used.

Strategies should be articulated with a specific dimension

---

[1] Arthur Waskow, "Looking Forward: 1999," *New University Thought,* VI, 3 (Spring, 1968), p. 34.

of social life in view. While broadside criticisms of society have some value in drawing attention to the basic nature of a problem, solutions must be problem-specific. It would not be feasible to explore here the multiple arenas of social experience that need examination. So that we may be problem-specific in this study, examples will be selected from the economic arena.

In order to imagine and create the future, Waskow suggests, one must work on a "practicable, desirable future." If we try to invent only the desirable future, he says, "it is likely to be much too 'far out' for effective pressure on the present society." Instead he writes:

> Just as this kind of future-building looks for the *possible* rather than either the replica of present or impossible though desirable future (impossible within a given time span) so it is an examination of the seriously *possible* rather than the most likely. Instead of being a prediction — that is, the author's best judgment of what present trends are likely to produce — it is what might be called a possidiction — that is, the author's projection of how certain seeds of change that exist already might be made to flourish, given certain kinds of political action. The possidiction describes worlds that are, say, 30% likely — as against either worlds that are only 1% likely or those that are 60% likely. There is a serious chance they can be brought into being, but it will take a lot of doing. And the possidiction acts as an incitement to the necessary action.[2]

Some seeds of change, some strategies, are already developing. A number of these will be examined and their desirability and direction commented upon. First we shall look at what is happening within large economic organizations, then turn to wider economic programs.

I. INDUSTRIAL ORGANIZATION STRATEGIES

A. UPGRADING VICTIMS OF RACISM

One of the first strategies used by industrial leadership in Detroit following the July 1967 rebellion was to focus on securing jobs for hard-core unemployed. In order to guarantee that the ghetto worker would be competitive with the

---

[2] *Ibid.*, p. 39.

white, industries set up training programs to upgrade workers so they could fit into the industrial environment. Since the rebellion, a flurry of activity has been directed at designing programs to train the hard-core unemployed. Some companies are doing this independently, without government assistance. Others are benefiting from government support. In either case, the strategy is clear — get black men or other victims of racism equipped to compete with whites for entry-level jobs in industry.

A second level of upgrading is also occurring. Some blacks, already in industry, are being upgraded through special training programs and then promoted. At lower levels in the organization, there is some attention being given to promotion procedure and advancement of blacks to higher positions of responsibility. It is clear, however, that in spite of policy pressure by the company, there is much foot-dragging in the whole promotion process.

These programs are necessary but not sufficient. Judging from conversations with men either directing the training or participating as trainees, there is little awareness of white institutional racism. It is quite clear that the focus remains on blacks as the problem. Both upgrading efforts are assimilationist. At best, they provide some equipping for self-determination of black people within a white organization. The equipping is of black individuals, however; and there is little enablement of new black consciousness and unified group action. In fact some programs include actions to reduce black consciousness to a minimum. Where, in some plants, trainees seeking to encourage self-respect or self-determination have placed pictures of Stokely Carmichael or Malcolm X in the training area, this move has been strongly resisted by white management. Blacks with beards, beads or Afro-American dress have been deliberately excluded from some training programs. Criteria for promotability are also problematic. Instead of promoting blacks who can work effectively with newly hired blacks, white managers often promote men most like themselves. This procedure, of course, puts the black man in an impossible position. Any credentials he may have had with black workers are quickly questioned. He is turned into a pawn for white power. Perhaps workers should have a greater voice in choosing their own foremen.

These white management tendencies do not appear to be isolated examples. Research of white institutional practices is needed to see how extensively these standards of acceptability are used to exclude blacks. It is not enough to deal with individual blacks; industry must learn how to affirm black power and black consciousness.

B. Changing Organizational Structure

Some companies have moved beyond upgrading and promotion. They have made minor modifications in their own organizational structure.

Prior to the 1967 rebellion in Detroit, a number of companies had very strict hiring and recruitment policies and procedures. Following the rebellion, a number of companies made shifts in policy and practice. Ford Motor Company, for example, sent recruiters to ghetto areas and changed company entrance requirements; e.g., they now accepted otherwise qualified men who had prison records. These moves recognized that blacks were not the only problem. White institutions had to change too.

Recently, another shift in organizational focus occurred. Many companies are concentrating on foremen as a major problem area. A number of foreman-training programs have been developed to equip them to deal with the new work force.

While these changes are necessary, they still are not sufficient. Modification of structures loosens assimilationist standards. However, these programs still imply that only those whites who have direct contact with the new work force must be changed. It remains easy for other managers to think they are not the problem. This is especially true when the company admits it is now operating on a double standard.

In efforts to be honest about hiring and promotion policies and to address the urban crisis directly, some companies publicly admit that they are practicing reverse discrimination. If two equally qualified men — one white and one black — are available for hiring and promotion to a particular job, the company admits it would hire and/or promote the black. We have also heard a few managers admit they would hire a less qualified black over a more qualified white. On the face of it, this company policy seems to be facing white racism clearly. In fact, it is not. The argument for a double standard conceals a racist assumption. Many white workers, when they hear this argument, angrily react. Why, they ask, is discrimination in reverse fair now when it was not fair before? Two wrongs don't make a right. These workers are right, but their orientation is wrong. This argument is usually advanced not to urge justice for blacks but to secure their own position.

Regardless of intention, argument for a double standard fails to address the real justice issue. It implies that whites who recognize the obvious injustice of a double standard are willing to violate their own principles to make room for a black work force. The blacks still come out as a problem. If blacks were not demanding entrance into the company, there would be no need for the double standard. The policy highlights white goodness, rather than facing white racism as the problem.

The real issue is equity or reparation, not an unjust double standard. Both equity and reparation clearly identify the problem. Perpetrators of injustice are obligated to make right a long-standing wrong. The issue of reparation, so prominent today because of the Black Manifesto, is extremely difficult if not impossible for whites to comprehend, because they misplace the problem. As long as whites believe blacks are the cause of racial upheaval no issue of reparation makes sense. However, within the context of new white consciousness there is a meaningful and fruitful conception to define a major aspect of white responsibility. White guilt, although unavoidably linked to reparation, is not the real issue. At stake rather is what whites stand for and do.

Today, these two strategies — upgrading the victims of racism and slightly changing organizational structures — appear to be the ones Detroit industry is using to deal with racism. Both are necessary but not sufficient. New white consciousness demands more. Two more changes are beginning to emerge. They offer brighter possibilities for a more extensive attack on cultural and institutional racism in industry.

C. Examining Racism in Organizations

Some whites in industry are beginning to recognize the depths of racism in America as a whole as well as in the industrial setting. This dawning awareness, this birth of new whiteness, is forcing them to raise different kinds of questions and press in new directions. It is apparent that men in many places and in some unlikely power positions are beginning to act.

One man who seriously struggled with the issue never before considered racism to be a problem in his department. He was preoccupied with the problems of alienation and frustration caused by a destructive bureaucracy. Since there were no black people in his department he thought racism was not a problem. Now he is beginning to wrestle with racism in a department that includes no blacks. He has begun to look at departmental promotion policy and examine the orientations by which members of his department understand the racial situation.

In another company, a group of men struggling to devise a multistage program to train managers to deal with hard-core employees have come to realize that the problem transcends hard-core employment. Foremen report to supervisors who in turn report to higher authorities, leading the group to realize that the problem penetrates the whole white-dominated structure. They are now developing a new stage in their program, designed to attack institutional racism in areas that do not include black people.

I know of only one major employer in Detroit — Michigan Bell Telephone — seriously embarking upon a total examination of racism. Some people are beginning to recognize that the whole organization must be radically open to the victims of racism *whether or not* blacks and others *want* to enter that organization. Liberal whites are going to have to struggle with the quasi-moral contention that blacks are not qualified for responsible positions. Conservative whites must take seriously the necessity for more equitable distribution of power.

The methodology for an extensive attack on institutional racism is beginning to develop. One company hired a team of new white researchers to investigate racism in their total operation. That research was then fed back to decision-makers in the company with recommendations for implementation and follow-through. In another company the racism inventory mentioned earlier (see Appendix) was used as a base for an extensive company examination of policies and practices. On the basis of insights gathered from that analysis, plus a training program on new whiteness, new policies and practices were instituted. Where racism is a part of the structure but not intentionally perpetuated, it must be intentionally stamped out— and it can be.

The only quesion is the will of the white leadership. Companies must not only be nonracist. They must be actively antiracist.

D. Pressing for Organizational Alternatives

New whites are not just against racism; they are for justice. As such, they are constantly searching for fuller expressions of self-determination, respect, and pluralism.

One seed of change arises from sources other than those dealing directly with racism. A great contribution to the elimination of racism and a wider building of viable organizational structure may result. Rooted in the behavioral sciences, these changes are coming to prominence through increased emphasis on organizational development. Companies are spending millions of dollars annually to secure advice and counsel of behavioral scientists in solving staggering organizational problems. Few aspects of organizational life escape the scrutiny of these consultants. As a result, many company leaders are beginning to understand that new forms of organizational life are required to deal with escalation of social and technical change.

One organizational consultant, Warren Bennis, argues that organizations will have to change if they expect to keep pace with rapid societal change. He suggests that organizational change will have to include:

1. Full and free communication, regardless of rank and power.
2. Reliance on consensus, rather than on the more customary forms of coercion or compromise, to manage conflict.
3. The idea that influence is based on technical con-

74

fidence and knowledge rather than on the vagaries of personal whims or prerogatives of power.

4. An atmosphere that permits and even encourages emotional expression as well as task-oriented acts.

5. A basically human bias, one which accepts the inevitability of conflict between the organization and the individual but which is willing to cope with and mediate this conflict on rational grounds.[3]

These kinds of changes will have tremendous effect on both black and white workers in the organization. Self-determination, respect, and pluralism will be greatly enhanced if organizations move from the present rigid bureaucratic model that dominates industry to one that is more flexible, open, and human.

Another area of behavioral science research beginning to have impact is the fresh examination of the nature of work. Frederick Herzberg, noted consultant and researcher, in his book *Work and the Nature of Man*[4] suggests that the job itself has not been sufficiently examined by behavioral science or industrial management. Very little has been done, Herzberg argues, to design work with built-in motivation. A few companies have begun to examine work itself and have developed experimental programs of job redesign.[5]

These two directions, work on the total organization and work on changing job structure, are the basis for more radical thought about the nature of American organizational life.

Blacks may or may not be pressing for these kinds of organizational alternatives. For many blacks, first on their agenda is breaking down the racism that has excluded them from organizational participation. The real radicals for organizational change may come not from the black community but from the white community. It is no accident that the middle-class affluent white society has spawned white radicals on campuses. Since survival is not a basic issue for

---

[3] Warren Bennis, *Changing Organizations* (N. Y., McGraw-Hill, 1966), p. 18.

[4] Frederick Herzberg, *Work and the Nature of Man* (Cleveland, World Publishing Company, 1966).

[5] Robert Terry, "Do You Like Your Work?" *Life and Work*, X, 3 (February 1968).

most whites, we have the opportunity, obligation, and need to imagine a new future and to work to make it a reality.

II. WIDER ECONOMIC STRATEGIES

Many strategies to deal with racism transcend internal organizational change. They range from black entrepreneurship or black capitalism to guaranteed annual income to a total revamping of the mixed market system.

Since many of the plans do not deal primarily with racism, focusing instead on redistribution of wealth, conglomerates, or other problems of justice, they will not be discussed in detail here. There is a great body of thoughtful literature out on any of these topics.

There are, however, two considerations that are relevant for antiracist whites. One is that whatever strategies are used, they should be judged by the results they produce for the masses of people of color. Whether redistributing power, opening institutions, or establishing new norms, the criterion of success is whether the new plans build in at the outset actual decision-making power for groups potentially affected by any plan, develop flexible and human organizations that are not oppressive, and strengthen norms that protect and enhance the integrity of the culture of the people for whom the plans are projected.

Concomitant with this suggestion is the second consideration. Proposals for wider economic alternatives that transcend the issues of racism call for fresh and penetrating analysis of "old white economic and political consciousness." Our inherent understanding of private property — whether it be a car or stock in General Motors — which suggests that we can treat all property similarly without regard to social impact, desperately needs reappraisal and change. Guaranteed annual income calls into question the "myth" of hard work and individual initiative as the only or major prerequisite for authentic societal and economic self-determination. Black entrepreneurship, besides raising questions of whether it redistributes wealth and power to masses of blacks, provides the opportunity for a long hard look at the results of white capitalism on whites.

The burden of proof is shifting today. Those who defend the American economic and political systems are now confronted with the hard fact — make those systems work justly for all or face their demise.

One way to get perspective on our own economic system is to engage in serious study of other economic systems. The economic system of Yugoslavia, Cuba, Sweden, or England might be examined in order to gain distance on our own. Exploration of alternatives does not necessarily dictate rejection of the American system. Examining other systems sharpens our capacity to analyze our own situation and to identify specific weaknesses that need correction.

In this section, following Waskow's advice, a notion of a desirable practicable future has been developed. He suggests that we must "work out as vividly and in as much detail as possible, the way in which that practicable desirable future would work and would look. And then you work backward from that, in a kind of retroactive projection, to see what kinds of change *in detail* would be necessary in order to get to that stage."[6] The detail work has not been done in this book. Each new white performs this task in his particular location and within his particular arena of power and expertise. Only the broad directions of change that have the potential of being translated into the desirable practicable future have been outlined. This is the first stage in what Waskow calls the method of success of approximation. By that he means the method through which "you move from analysis of change of the future and back again, back and forth as many times as you like, getting more and more detail each time."[7]

---

[6] Waskow, p. 40.

[7] *Ibid.*

CHAPTER V

TACTICS FOR CHANGE

Strategy requires implementation. Change tactics are necessary to guarantee the elimination of racism and the construction of a more just society. In any discussion of tactics, two questions immediately arise: What tactics (means) are justifiable? What tactics are appropriate and effective? Let us look at each of these in turn, assuming that the answers to the two questions are not the same.

I. WHAT TACTICS ARE JUSTIFIABLE?

Recently, in a discussion of new white and black consciousness, one man noted a Malcolm X button bearing the phrase "Freedom by whatever means necessary." He pointed at the button and said loudly, "I can't support that!" To most whites and many blacks, the phrase "By whatever means necessary" signals physical violence. It is difficult to convince them that the phrase points to absolute commitment. It is equally hard to get them to understand that the means employed by blacks and new whites depend upon the amount of old white resistance to change.

New whites cannot tolerate a racist society. What means are justifiable to eliminate that racism? At least three types of problems are raised by this question: Is nonviolence a clear option? Doesn't violence violate due process? And, does persistent resistance to groups of people, not just individuals, change the definition of the situation to justify more radical means?

Joseph Hough, university professor and social analyst, has written a provocative and useful article on justifiable violence. He identifies six types of violence with which Americans are preoccupied. Vietnam, he suggests, is the most obvious, closely followed by concern with violent crime. Political figures, as well as the man on the street, are acutely aware of the growing incidence of violent crimes. Many feel criminal violence is out of control. Although these two forms of violence assume great importance, the last four that Hough describes are especially relevant to the new white. Hough writes:

> There is what has been referred to as "systematic," "structural," or "figurative" violence. Into this category are lumped all the effects of unjust social systems upon those who are at the bottom of the social scale. This has been especially a concern of non-white groups whose position in American society has been determined by systematic discrimination in a creation of inferior life chances in a segregated society.[1]

This is, of course, what we referred to as institutional racism. White society, through its injustice, has been structurally violent to the human beings trapped by institutions.

> A fourth category of violence that is of concern to the nation might be labeled civil disturbance. This is usually a response to structural violence that involves burning, looting, and some attacks on persons. However, it has been demonstrated by the analysis in the Kerner Report, this type of violence is seldom a planned strategy. As we shall see later, it may be used strategically but does not begin with any type of conspiratorial action.[2]

In America, as well as other countries, civil disturbance is often intensified by overreaction by police and other law enforcement agencies. This overreaction is the fifth type of violence that Hough points out. "Police violence occurs," he says, "when more force is employed than is necessary to contain a civil disorder, or when excessive force is used as an 'example to others who might be contemplating some kind of disruption.' "[3] Just as the Kerner Report pointed to

---

[1] Joseph Hough, Jr., "The Christian, Violence and Social Change," a lecture given at School of Theology at Claremont, January, 1969, p. 1.

[2] *Ibid.*

[3] *Ibid.*, pp. 1-2.

the structural violence perpetrated by white society on blacks, police violence was documented by the Daniel Walker Report.[4]

A sixth type, revolutionary violence, is also drawing the attention of most Americans. Hough distinguishes civil disturbance from revolutionary violence. The latter, he feels, is "planned as strategy for social change, and the violent acts are calculated to effect a certain response from the established forces."[5] Although the distinction between civil disturbance and revolutionary violence is difficult to make,[6] it must be made because there are important differences in the two kinds. Some of the clearest examples of revolutionary violence are on college campuses, where destruction is planned with certain specific goals in mind.

The question before the new white is whether he is ever justified in using revolutionary violence as a tactic.

His options are not simply violence and nonviolence. The real choice is whether the new white is willing to acquiesce to structural violence or creatively use some other form of violence to combat it. What many of us are learning is that violence cannot be avoided in a racist society. We are either perpetrators of structural violence through inaction or builders of a just society through appropriate means. Not every action taken must be violent. On the contrary, alternative forms of action are available and workable. What this analysis suggests is that by avoiding the deeper implications of structural violence, we can be deluded into thinking that no form of violence is ever justifiable.[7] Facile appeals to due process will not do. Grappling with the power held by white institutions leads to the sober realization that radical means may be necessary to deal with the radical white problem. Only with this view can we adequately assess the variety of

---

[4] *Rights in Conflict* (N. Y., Bantam Books, 1968). A report submitted by Daniel Walker, Director of the Chicago Study Team, to the National Commission on the Causes and Prevention of Violence.

[5] Hough, p. 2.

[6] Since civil disturbance is not planned, it is not included as a tactic. However, new whites might at some time have to decide whether or not to join a civil disturbance once one has begun.

[7] See George Coe and Kirby Page, "Violence, Non-Violence and the Uses of Coercion," in *The Quiet Battle,* edited by Mulford Sibley (N. Y., Anchor Books, 1963).

legitimate means available to deal with this acute situation.

The possibility of revolutionary violence as an integral alternative grows out of deep frustration and disillusionment with traditional means of achieving justice. Most whites, caught up in middle-class security, fail to realize the forces of resistance to social change. Popular thought holds that justice can be brought about legally through the courts, politically by voting, and economically by selective buying. In other words, the basic mechanisms of the American system — the courts, the political process, and the market system — are equitable mechanisms that only demand use to be effective. What this analysis fails to uncover is the tremendous power advantage of those within the system versus the powerlessness of those excluded. At times, violent gestures seem necessary if the attention of constituted powers is to be directed toward problems in society and action is to be effected.

Since we have been drawing examples from the economic arena, let us take a brief look at labor-management history to illustrate the problems of due process, and structural and intentional uses of violence. This historical perspective is especially important for labor and management leadership, who seem to have short memories.

Joseph Rayback, respected chronicler of labor history, describes some of the basic patterns in the strikes at the turn of the century:

> The conflicts followed a remarkably similar pattern. Regardless of instigation, the miners in almost every strike were quickly confronted with a determined and ruthless employer front which created citizens' alliances to harry strikers with credit boycotts and beatings, which hired strike breakers and armed guards, and forced local authorities to recruit deputies to "protect private property." Most every conflict became, at some time during its history, a miniature war with guards and deputy sheriffs — organized at times even into machine gun and cavalry divisions — facing equally well organized strikers. The terrorization of the local population by armed guards and deputies and the dynamiting of company property, by parties unknown, were common features of every strike. When company and local resources failed, employers persuaded state authorities to dispatch the militia to restore "law and

order." With the militia came the removal of local officials sympathetic to the strikers, erection of bull pens, the incarceration of strikers and their friends, elaborate blacklist systems, and deportations.[8]

Later in the same chapter Rayback discusses some of the important contributions of the Industrial Workers of the World (IWW), known also as the Wobblies. Says Rayback,

> its [the Wobblies] campaigns revealed, contrary to AFL philosophy, that the migratory, casual, unskilled laborers, with their diverse languages, customs, prejudices, religions, and animosities, were organizable. More significant was the impact of the Wobbly campaigns on the "progressives." Wobbly strikes revealed how thoroughly industry controlled the local governments, and how willing it was to use its control with a brutal velocity that gave no regard to civil rights. This made a lasting impression upon men who believed implicitly in democratic process as the surest technique for solving all the nation's problems; it made them friends of labor because the laboring men were being denied their basic democratic rights. The strikes also revealed that a very large segment of the laboring population was living under deplorable economic circumstances in the midst of splendor.[9]

Labor history reflects illustration after illustration of the governmental shifts from collusion with management to support of labor and then back again. Violence marked much of labor history. Although some labor leaders today romanticize their past and suggest that labor only attacked property and never persons, there is clear evidence that labor's operational credo was, "We shall get recognition by whatever means necessary." That recognition was slow in coming. Democratic machinery was excruciatingly slow to recognize labor's right to exist. It was not until July 1935, with passage of the Wagner Act, that labor secured its rightful place as a legitimate structure in American society. However, in spite of that law, industry continued to use violent

[8] Joseph Rayback, *A History of American Labor* (N. Y., Free Press, 1959), p. 234.

[9] *Ibid.,* p. 249.

[10] During 1936-37 the Lafollette Civil Liberties Committee was formed to investigate the methods used by industry to combat the union. Rayback cites how weapons such as tear gas, grenades and

methods to combat unionism.[10] A reading of labor history presents the awesome question of who is really violent in America. Labor's intentional violence seems minuscule compared with the structural violence perpetrated against it.

Today the power alignment is different. Labor, no longer an underdog seeking to gain recognition and power, is aligned with management as a perpetrator of structural violence on minority racial groups, especially blacks. The rearrangement of power, however, has not changed the tactics of the powerful. Reading labor history is like reading the morning newspaper. The reactions are the same, only the actors have been changed.

The United Auto Workers' response to DRUM (Dodge Revolutionary Union Movement) is a good case in point. The tragedy is that the white-dominated UAW thinks it is not the problem. It prides itself on its many battles on behalf of victims of injustice. In the letter cited earlier in which the UAW clarified its stand against "divisive groups," the UAW rehearsed its credentials:

> The UAW throughout its history has taken its stand firmly in support of the struggle for justice, for equal rights and equal opportunity to all people. UAW leaders and members have been in the vanguard of the legislative fight for civil rights. We have marched in Detroit, in Washington, D.C., Selma, Alabama, Jackson, Mississippi, Memphis, Tennessee, for justice and equity.[11]

The letter also notes several ways in which the UAW has been involved in community projects:

> We have been in the leadership in the crusade against poverty. We have worked to help provide housing for low income families, to improve police-community relations, to establish community unions, to create job training programs and pre-apprenticeship programs for the disadvantaged, to improve our educational system particularly in the inner-city area, to ensure equal rights and equal op-

---

shells were used during the Little Steel Strike of 1937, when Youngstown Sheet and Tube and Republic Steel "employed a uniformed police force of 400 men equipped with revolvers, rifles, shot guns and tear gas, which they 'used to shoot down citizens on the streets and highways' during the strike" (p. 343).

[11] Letter from the UAW International Executive Board, March 10, 1969.

portunities in the factories and also to bring to fruition the freedom, the self-respect, the dignity and the good life to all people which a democratic society can provide.[12]

It is clear from reading the UAW letter and other publications produced by Solidarity House that the UAW envisions itself as the leader in bringing about social justice in the United States. Yet, sadly, it fails to recognize or admit the racism within its own organization. It is more concerned with denying DRUM and other black groups an appropriate voice in redressing the injustices within the UAW and within Chrysler Corporation than it is in examining its own house. The UAW continually argues that its own due process is workable but fails to admit the possibility that "due process" can be used for injustice as well. The UAW was founded on the principle that men have the right to organize for power to redress injustice. However, it refuses that right to its own workers who are attempting to organize for power to fight injustice within the union. The UAW consciousness is basically white liberal. It presupposes that it is healthy and from that presupposition seeks to minister to sickness. Only when the UAW begins to take a hard look at its own structure and the racism within it will it be able to redress the just demands of its black members.

Although it is a sad commentary on the responsiveness of our major institutions, past and present American experience clearly shows that warnings by victims of injustice, ethicists, and social scientists count for little in social change. Institutions change under pressure. Racist institutions seem to require greater pressure, even violence, to change.

Persistent white resistance to fundamental claims for justice by large groups of people creates a potentially revolutionary situation. Such a situation becomes more akin to war than to mere redress of personal grievances. The issues become self-determination of people (not just of individuals), independent political and economic structures, and a radical consciousness pressing new norms or recalling old norms that received lip service in the past. At such a time, the following words are appropriate:

When in the course of human events it becomes necessary

---

[12] *Ibid.*

for one people to dissolve the political bonds which have connected them with another, and to assume among the powers of the earth the separate and equal station to which the laws of nature and of nature's God entitle them, a decent respect to the opinions of mankind requires that they should declare the causes which impel them to the separation.

We hold these truths to be self-evident: that all men are created equal; that they are endowed by their Creator with certain unalienable rights; that among these are life, liberty, and the pursuit of happiness; that to secure these rights, governments are instituted among men, deriving their just powers from the consent of the governed; that whenever any form of government becomes destructive of these ends, it is the right of the people to alter or abolish it, and to institute new government, laying its foundation on such principles, and organizing its power in such form as to them shall seem most likely to effect their safety and happiness.

Violence as a tactic, although justifiable in some instances, never brings unmixed blessings; intentional violence triggers repression.[13] Government and management formed a united front against labor to repress labor's demands in the past. Already today, we see many overreactions to pending demands for justice. Violence has the potential of being counterproductive, acting to solidify the status quo rather than change it.

Revolutionary violence also risks the danger of romanticization. Very few Americans have ever experienced the bloody reality of a revolution. Instead, most of us have participated in its rhetoric. Sometimes it is easy to get the feeling that the talk of revolutionary violence by whites is more a catharsis for white guilt than it is an intentional strategy of change. Violence can be suicidal as well as productive.

Finally, a serious danger in violent activity is that the cause for which violence is designed may be unjust and demonic. The new white is continually pressed to match means with ends and ends with means. He needs clarity about both so that he can see that the means are appropriate to the end; that the end in fact justifies the means.

---

13 See *Repression in America* distributed by PAR.

II. *WHAT TACTICS ARE APPROPRIATE AND EFFECTIVE?*

It is the wise man who can match tactics with goals and strategy in any given situation. It is the effective man who possesses more than one tactic. What then are appropriate, effective tactics to change institutions and cultures?

A. DIALOGUE

The most readily available and mildest tactic for any new white is dialogue. This tactic is particularly effective to change people who are on the fence, who need support for new thought, or who are seriously trying to make sense out of their deepest commitments. It is less effective for those whose mind is strongly made up in an opposite direction. A dialogue tactic has available to it various methods for effectively presenting material. Films, other visual aids, buzz groups and panels are all common.

This tactic was the initial one used by the New Detroit Committee when it set up its volunteer speakers bureau. Originally, the speakers bureau aimed at training men and women to interpret the urban crisis. Its target was primarily white groups but also interested black groups. The task of the speaker was to suggest alternative ways of understanding the present, to challenge the participants to begin to move to attack white racism in their own communities, and to mobilize power necessary to produce change.

Most of the speakers confronting white groups learned two things. First, a white talking to whites about racism quickly finds the conversation turning to blacks as the problem. White speakers found it extremely difficult to get whites to talk about themselves as the root cause of racial unrest. Second, whites dealing with a white audience found it almost impossible to report the meaning and impact of racism on the black community without blacks being present. The discussion had more impact if a white and black team confronted the white audience. The team had to work together so white audiences could not center on blacks. The constant temptation for many blacks is to be seduced by the white question — What do you want? Instead, the team throws the question back to the audience and asks them, What do you want?

Dialogue as a tactic should be a regular tool of the new white, to be used with neighbors, friends, and any institutional setting. Though it is one of the mildest tactics that can be used, there is risk involved. A number of New Detroit speakers have found that their suburban friends no longer invite them to social gatherings or to their homes. A number of them have felt isolation and loneliness because they have been ostracized by their own community. One antidote to this ostracism is to organize a cadre of new whites.

B. CONFRONTATION

A second tactic, designed to be stronger than dialogue, is confrontation. An example of this approach was a session recently conducted by the New Detroit Speakers Bureau to train new speakers. A number of black and white consultants trained in group work, as well as black and white consciousness, designed a training session that included confrontation. Three content areas were programmed into the two-day event — black consciousness, white institutional racism, and new white consciousness. Following each major presentation a two-and-a-half-hour small group session was held. The plan called for the major learning experience to occur in the small groups. In order to facilitate that process, a black and white team was assigned to lead each group, one of the leaders being particularly skilled in one of the content areas and the other skilled in group process.

About a day and a half into the conference, the blacks called a caucus. All the blacks left to go to another room while the whites sat alone in the lecture hall — stunned and bewildered. Some whites were suspicious that the caucus had been planned by the leadership. Others were upset that blacks and whites were separated. In reality, the caucus was not premeditated but grew out of the dynamics of the meeting. But it forced the whites to come to terms with themselves in a way that they never had done before.

The agenda for the rest of the day was cancelled and the whites had to create their own agenda for the remainder of the afternoon. One group of whites was so shattered by the day-and-a-half experience that they formed themselves into the "125 Percent Shattered Group" to try to make some sense out of what was happening. Other whites formed into small intense discussion groups dealing with institutional racism and new white consciousness. One group formed a discussion to figure out procedures by which to deal with the possible demands from the black caucus.

Two hours after the black caucus convened, they returned to place their demands before the total meeting. They did not ask for white support. Rather they said they would work in the speakers bureau, but they also demanded a hearing before the Board of Directors of the New Detroit Committee to confront that board with the racism within the organization itself.

The whites were forced into a dilemma. What should they do with the demand of the black caucus? Should they simply let it be read? Should they support it? Should they write their own amendment to it? After much hassling and public debate, the white caucus finally supported the demand, promising to work to guarantee the hearing before the Board of Directors and also independently or together with the black caucus to work to eliminate racism at New Detroit, Incorporated.

This confrontation between black and white was agonizing for many whites. Most had never been in this kind of situation. Many had never met or talked with articulate, middle-class, angry blacks. The overall result of this kind of confrontation was extremely valuable and useful. Of the eighty-four whites in attendance, at least 80 percent responded positively to this confrontation and deepened their own insight, understanding, and commitment to fight racism as a result of it. Some whites were extremely threatened by the event and reacted with great hostility. In balance, the designers of the conference felt that the confrontation tactic was a valuable tool for change, especially change of consciousness.

Two modifications of the confrontation design are a straight sensitivity group approach and an exposure approach. The sensitivity approach to change requires skilled leadership and fairly deep commitments by members to engage in this form of activity. There are many options in sensitivity training, from an unstructured approach to a more structured approach. In the unstructured approach the trainer and group begin in silence until someone begins to speak. That speaking, along with others' responses, then becomes the grist for the confrontation. The more structured sensitivity group approach may include exercises that the leader designs for the group in order more rapidly to get data out on the table for group interaction.

A second modification of confrontation is exposure. This design is based on the premise that whites cannot begin to deal with their own racism until they are exposed to the demonic results of that racism. Detroit Industrial Mission was asked by one of the auto companies to design a one-day urban plunge for various management personnel in their company who were having to deal directly with the urban crisis. The Mission designed a day of exposure and reflection. The exposure was primarily to the black community, the reflection primarily upon white racism as the problem.

The Mission staff arranged confrontations between auto executives and ADC mothers, welfare administrators, an articulate new left spokesman, a militant community organization, and a funding agency for black entrepreneurship. The management group was divided into teams of five men and a young black militant guide. The guide accompanied the team of five men throughout the day, responding to their questions and pressing them about the seriousness and depth of "the problem." At the end of the day, all the teams returned for an hour-and-a-half debriefing with a black and white team from the Mission. The task — confront the white problem. For most of the managers this was a shock since their assumption was that they as whites were there to help blacks with the "black problem." Some of the managers could not accept that they were the problem. Many, however, began to see and hear things with a radically new understanding. The feedback from the participants again and again cited the one-day urban plunge as a highlight of their week of training. There they began to get some inkling of the seriousness and depth of the issues and their organization's pervasive involvement in setting up the problems. Within that perspective they felt they might begin far-reaching solutions.

During this year, we at Detroit Industrial Mission have learned that confrontation of whites by blacks is an ineffective tactic if not accompanied by new white analysis. The confrontation heightens white guilt, defensiveness, and anger. This white response is not necessarily bad. However, the confrontation by itself provides no way for whites to make sense out of black rage or their own responses. Therefore, in any confrontation training design, we include a major block of time for struggle with new whiteness.

Presently the Mission's design consists of three parts: black consciousness, new white consciousness, and testing. Testing was added most recently because we felt that mere exposure to new white consciousness was inadequate. New whiteness had to be internalized and acted out in new forms of behavior. At each point in the training design the Mission has had to face the problem of uniting theoretical clarity with "gut" feeling. Neither theory divorced from experience nor experience unclarified by theory will do. Both theory and experience had to unite and lead to a new understanding and new forms of action.

C. RESEARCH AND FEEDBACK

Earlier we mentioned the possibility of outside teams or teams of new whites internal to the organization engaging in extensive research on racism. That information, along with data on policy implementation, should be fed back to the management team for implementation. This approach is a basic method used by the Committee for One Society in Chicago — a group that devised and has used the inventory on racism. It has the advantage of providing a comprehensive look at racism in the corporation but can have the disadvantage of not following through to implementation. If the research is done by groups inside the organization, then follow-through could be built into the design.

D. ECONOMIC PRESSURE

The fifth tactic is selective economic pressure. Operation Breadbasket in Chicago is perhaps the best illustration of the economic boycott as a tactic to fight racism. New whites can learn the potential power of economic boycotts from this black-run operation. Boycotts are not easy to organize or administer, but with clear targets and a strong organizational base they can be effective. They raise few questions of legality and generally do not conflict with the law.

Along with boycotts there are other forms of economic pressure, such as adverse publicity to corporations through the mass media, comparative buying in ghetto and suburban stores to place pressure on chain stores to maintain unity of prices, picketing of particular locations to draw attention to particular problems, and even internal harassment of stores, such as by leaving large quantities of food unbought in shopping baskets or on checkout counters.

E. Inside-Outside Alliance

Often groups seeking change feel that they have either to attack an institution from the outside and risk ineffectiveness and alienation, or become part of the institution and risk ineffectiveness and assimilation. However, if we grant that not all new whites will ever agree on similar tactics and that no one tactic is necessarily appropriate for all new whites in any given situation, then a sixth possibility for change is feasible.

Radical tactics, often sustained by an outside militant group, can provide the opening wedge for equally militant insiders to use more moderate tactics to secure solid advances. An insider in an organization often needs a bargaining point that he can use as a lever to move someone or some practice. Without it, he is often immobilized.

Insiders and outsiders do not need to confer secretly on joint action programs, although they might. Rather, each group can take full advantage of the other's efforts and thereby spur each other on. Instead of insiders despairing over having to solve another social problem, they could as new whites use problems as pain-signaling events to initiate change. Likewise, instead of outsiders thinking they are going it alone, they could as new whites take courage that sustained gains are being made through more radical tactics. Of course, whether this strategy works depends on whether or not new white consciousness is an integral part of both insiders and outsiders.

F. Attack on Property and Person

It is deeply disturbing to face the necessity of attacking property to secure justice. It is tragic to consider attacking persons. Neither can be considered lightly; the consequences

91

are momentous. Of the two, certainly property destruction is infinitely less important than human destruction.

The judgment of whether or not these tactics may be necessary depends upon societal and institutional resistance to change. New whites will have to engage in the most thoughtful and sensitive analysis of societal and institutional resistance and develop guidelines that specify under what conditions focused violence would be an appropriate tactic. We have not attempted to identify particular societal and institutional points of resistance. It is impossible to make those kinds of judgments divorced from the particular situations that call for action. At this point, all we can say is that these tactics may be necessary. If all other avenues for change fail to dislodge racism, then more radical means must be employed.

Regardless of tactics used, one final point should be stressed. The tactics used to change institutions are not necessarily the same as those used to change consciousness. Economic or political pressures, for example, may be effective for institutional change. Confrontations of black and white combined with lecture may be more effective for changing consciousness. Tactics must be tailored to *what* is being changed. To change attitudes may even require other tactics. From what has been learned, no one tactic is totally sufficient. We live under the demand to develop multiple tactics and use them wisely and creatively.

CHAPTER VI

PERSONAL STYLES FOR NEW WHITES

A brief look will be taken at characteristics of personal styles that seem required of the new white. By style is meant the way we translate new whiteness into action. We are just beginning to discover some of the parameters of the emerging style for new whites, and many of these remarks are exploratory and suggestive rather than conclusive.

I. POLITICAL

The first and perhaps dominant characteristic of style becomes obvious in the light of our analysis in the previous chapter. To be a new white means to become *intentionally political* — to use power creatively and justly. There is little question that new whites must become conscious of the power arrangements about them and the multiple uses of that power, and must recognize their own power potential. Frank Joyce rightly suggests that "anti-racist whites must first recognize their own powerlessness, particularly as individuals, to take on situations. They must, therefore, organize themselves and others. They must build a base."[1] To be unpolitical or apolitical is to be ineffective and socially impotent.

In a large manufacturing company in Detroit, a supervisor became convinced that his company had to translate its public policies against racism into practice. However, he felt that management levels above him were satisfied with the present policy and action. Through a number of strategic

---

[1] Joyce, "Introduction, Definition and Analysis," unpublished paper of People Against Racism, p. 7.

conversations and moves, this lower-line manager was able to convince a second-level manager (higher up in the organization) to attend a seminar on institutional racism. The seminar had sufficient influence on the top-line supervisor that he returned to his plant with a new understanding of racism in his own company. He was ready to move. Presently, the lower-line manager and top manager are working in concert to give new direction and implementation to company policies. They have become political and are beginning to be effective.

II. INTELLIGENT REFLECTION

The second dimension of style is the capacity for new whites to engage in *intelligent reflection*. Action and reflection upon that action must go hand in hand. Cadres of new whites can engage in serious depth analysis of institutions in which they are working. Faulty analysis yields ineffective action, but analysis without action yields empty thought. These efforts at reflection keep strategy and tactics aligned with the changing cultural and institutional situations. There is nothing worse than outdated action in an unrecognized, changed milieu.

III. NEW CREDENTIALS

A third dimension of personal style is the development of *credentials*. In black-white confrontation, whites tend to get into the role of evaluating black progress without having credentials to engage in such activity. Whites have not developed their own credentials by fighting against white racism. Not only will blacks reject whites in this "evaluative" role but whites have no business being in that role. New whites develop credentials to talk with blacks when new whites develop their own strategies, have their own failures, and are struggling to chart their directions. This does not mean that the new white has continually to recite what he has done. It will become apparent to any other new white or black whether the white has been fighting racism. The kinds of questions and issues that are of concern to him will send clear signals.

It has been my experience that only *after* whites have begun to work on racism can they begin to enter into significant conversations with blacks on the race question.

Whites often want prematurely to affiliate with blacks on race issues without having begun to attack racism in the white-dominated structures. If they try to make that premature affiliation they will find that they will most likely be reprimanded by blacks for their lack of involvement. Whites get their credentials from their fight with racism. Blacks have their credentials by being victims of racism. Once whites have begun to act in a concerted and continual effort to combat white racism, then and perhaps only then are they in a position to engage in serious conversation with blacks about the best methods and resources to engage in that task.

I have recently been working as consultant in a situation that vividly demonstrates this point. A Detroit-based, predominantly white group of churches has within the past year spawned a black militant community organization. The board found itself in the awkward position of being the policy board for the black organization. The history of that board, since it created and financed the militant organization, had yielded a series of deeply frustrating and agonizing confrontations between black militant leadership and white directors. There seemed to be no way to escape from charge and countercharge. Only recently has the board begun to realize the depth of suspicion between black and white and the untenable arrangement that had been spawned. White board members became convinced that they had no business being on a board of directors for a black organization and they encouraged development of a black board of directors for the militant organization. Furthermore, after struggle and probing, they also realized that to press a black board on the black group without committing themselves to the struggle against white racism was just another form of racism. What that action would have implied was that the black man could fight racism and the whites could go on with business as usual. Now the predominantly white board is struggling with its own strategy and tactics to deal with cultural, institutional, and individual racism. The hope is that as they become more actively engaged in the attack upon racism in their own organization they will then be in a position to work creatively with blacks on a peer relation rather than from the present defensive, impotent, or paternalistic stance.

The question of white credentials is emerging as an extremely important one, with ramifications far beyond what I had originally thought. Suspicion and hostility between blacks and whites is so great that efforts by whites to overcome that split on the basis of personal relationships are almost fruitless. Militant and even not so militant blacks will take every opportunity to make demands upon whites, castigate them for their racism, and instruct them on the demonic effects of their inaction. By and large, experience has shown that blacks are usually right in their criticisms. The only way for whites to get into the conversation is for them to admit that they are racists, and to commit themselves to attack racism and begin the arduous task of working to eliminate it. New whites and blacks can talk and work together when each is working against a common enemy.

IV. PROGRESSIVE LISTENING

The new white must be an aggressive listener. If we have begun to struggle deeply with some of the issues outlined in this essay, we have already made the first step in coming to understand the ravages of racism and the desperate necessity to eliminate it. We are also just beginning to understand that an antiracist society still has fundamental problems that must be overcome if all of us are to move forward creatively and humanely. New whites are willing to doubt the undoubted and ask hard questions as well as easy ones. We can take little for granted. We need to read in black literature as well as white literature. As best we can, we must know the demonic results of racism as well as what it means to be a perpetrator of racism.

Aggressive listening tests out what is being heard. There is the continual checking to make sure that what is heard is the same as what is intended in the conversation. Gesture and response need to be completed in shared meaning. Aggressive listening confirms the shared meaning. Effective political action and pertinent reflection are based in large measure on the depth and creativity of aggressive listening. Thus, although it is mentioned last in our discussion of personal style, in many ways aggressive listening is the foundation of growth and change for all of us.

*   *   *

CONCLUSION

The white community has the desperate need and opportunity to develop a new white consciousness. A growing readiness is apparent in the white community for this kind of analysis and these kinds of suggestions. The old models that whites have used to understand what has been going on in the urban crisis are inadequate. The new models that are being devised can bring a new coherence, direction, and stimulus for effective action. The new white committed to justice and working to rid this nation of its racism can be a major force for social change. The time is right. It is up to us to seize that time to turn our legacy of old white privilege into new white possibility.

ADDENDUM -
TRAPS FOR THE NEW WHITE

Already, as I have begun discussing this idea with the people in the wider Detroit community, I have found that there are subtle traps to be aware of in dealing with this kind of material.

The first is the danger of the *one best way*. Some groups working on racism have settled on one particular method-ology of change as an absolute. Experience has shown that, at this point in our history, we do not know enough about how to change institutions or cultures to permit the luxury of only one way. In the concern for direct action there is a tendency to be seduced into finding one method rather than being open to exploring a variety of methods. For example, some groups fighting racism believe that only whites should deal with whites and only blacks deal with blacks. It has been my experience that this is an ideological commitment rather than an effective tactic for change. I recognize the ideological point — whites must deal with their own problems rather than treating blacks as the prob-lem. However, I feel it is false to assume that only whites can do the job. Black and white teams seem to be more effective than whites alone. We need more empirical data before we can be sure that one way is necessarily better than another.

Second, some people are quick to pick up the label of new whiteness and avoid the struggle with its reality. As a result, new whiteness becomes a subtle guise for perpetuat-ing old thought forms and old styles of action. I have become wary of anyone who eagerly picks up the language without personal struggle or testing the new language against old behavior.

Third, I have come to the not too shocking conclusion that people are at various stages along the way in their struggle with the urban crisis. For many people new whiteness as a concept is not comprehensible. New whiteness, presented in its bald form, without an opportunity for people to understand that whiteness is the problem, fails to grasp the meaning or significance of the whole discussion. Presentations of this material are being tailored to the audience in such a way that they can receive and hear where they are rather than where I expect them to be. I have erred on this many times and am learning the hard way how to make these kinds of judgments.

Fourth, I have learned that rhetoric is often a smoke screen to disguise inaction. I have found many whites who are acting courageously in their own community in fighting racism but who do not possess the rhetoric to justify that activity. On the other hand, I find some individuals and groups using tremendous revolutionary rhetoric but showing few results for all the talk. We must not only listen to what someone says but also investigate what they are doing to get a true picture. The time for the romance of rhetoric is gone. We need solid analysis, focus, concern, and sustained action.

Fifth, the focus on whites as the problem may suggest a false solution. By implication, when we suggest "the white problem" as the cause, we also suggest that the whites are the solution. It is true that the white community is the root of the problem, but the whole community — white, black, red, brown, yellow — must be deeply involved in any solution. Justice requires it; our times require it.

Finally, there is the trap of self-righteousness. Granted, we must accept that the goal we are struggling for is sound and worth maximum effort. Nevertheless, we can defeat ourselves if we fail periodically to look at where we have been and where we are going. It is easy for us to become so enamored of ourselves and our own virtue that we miss the truth all about us. Openness need not undermine commitment; commitment should not blind us to new insight.

APPENDIX

INVENTORY OF RACISM

Committee for One Society
40 N. Ashland Avenue
Chicago, Ill.

Alvin Pitcher, Director
Susan Tobias, Director of Research
INVENTORY OF RACISM: How to Look for Institutional Racism.

I. Employment:

What percentage of workers are black? white? male? female? at each job level?

How are employees recruited? Does company have stated policy regarding equal employment opportunity? What is it? Is it publicized within the company? in the community? Is an employment agency used? Where are openings announced? Are openings announced to current employees only? Are openings in higher levels made known to present employees? Are jobs advertised in news media? in black community news media? What is turnover? black? white? Does the company use or have an employment center in the ghetto? Is there an aggressive policy — visiting high schools, scholarships and job promises made to students in high schools and colleges if students engage in particular programs?

What kind of application is used? Does it contain discriminatory and/or unnecessary questions?

Who does the interviewing? black or white persons? What training does the personnel director have in dealing with and understanding different peoples?

What are the criteria for different jobs? Are they objectively and consistently used? Are they written down? Can they be written down? If not, why not?

What are salaries at each job level? Are they uniform among employees at each level?

100

How are people promoted within the company? Are there mechanisms set up to train for promotion? Who get information about promotion? Is promotion a possibility for all employees? Is promotion a formal process or is it the result of social contacts? Who ride together to work? Who eat lunch together? Do employees belong to social clubs, etc. outside of company where company business gets done? What kind of special coaching and counseling is provided? Is special counseling provided to help black employees face problems of competition with more aggressive and prejudiced white employees? Is company and/or union newspaper used to announce new jobs, programs, promotions? What kinds of images are projected in newspaper? Who writes it? art work? Who prints it? Is information about training opportunities, etc. put up on company bulletin board?

What kinds of facilities are there for workers? recreational clubs? teams? Where do they play? Where are company picnics held? Who come?

Who makes final decisions on hiring and upgrading?

Are tests used to screen job applicants? Are tests equitable for blacks and whites? in results? What are patterns of test scores for different groups? Who made up tests? Have they been locally validated? Who administers tests? Who scores tests? Are employees tested on the job, e.g., using the machine they will be hired to operate? Are all applicants tested on the same machine? Do tests examine qualified or qualifiables? Is there on-the-job training? for whom? How are people recruited for it? Who runs training? Are supervisors trained to be sensitive to minority workers? What types of jobs are people trained for? Are jobs marginal or subject to elimination by automation?

What are employment benefits? Do all workers receive them? Is it policy to acquaint all employees with health insurance programs, for example? Do executives get stock options? social club memberships?

Is entry possible at all levels or must everyone come up through the ranks?

II. Are Black Suppliers and Services Used?
scavengers?
exterminators?
janitorial services?
office supplies?
accounting?
lawyers? doctors?

contractors?
answering service?
window washing?
banking? (including mortgages and loans)
insurances?
food products? (milk, orange juice, etc.)
maintenance supplies? (wax, bleach, etc.)

III. Investments:
What property is owned? Is property rented? for how much?
What are policies of firms renting in areas here discussed? Other investments?
Who handles portfolio? through what bank or finance company?
Who owns stock in company? in what amounts? Who are stockholders? Where do they live?
What are the policies of the companies in which investments are made — in areas under consideration here? employment? use of black services, etc.?
What are policies of white suppliers in areas considered here?

IV. Advertising:
What company is employed? kind of contract? size of account?
Models employed? images projected? of product? company? society?
Where is advertising done? what media used? in what communities?
Who does public relations work? Where is work done? How important is advertising? What proportion of business is invested there?
Who is advertising aimed at?
Are black images projected in black media or in all media? What are policies in employment, use of black services, etc.?
All supplies of services and materials should be examined in a similar way?
What does the primary company under examination do to influence policies of suppliers?

V. Government:
Is federal government involved in business or program? through what agency locally? How was it obtained? How is it used?

Does institution receive special consideration from government locally?

Who is alderman, congressman, etc.? Who represents area institution is based in?

Does institution depend on "good" relationship with public officials? Who?

VI. Board of Directors and Others:

Who is on board of directors? Who are officers?

What other boards do they sit on?

What social clubs do members belong to? voluntary associations?

What do members get paid per meeting?

Do members own significant portion of stock in company?

What other companies do members own stock in?

Do directors receive special stock options? What are they?

How does one get on the board? How long do they sit on it?

Is board important in setting policy or only rubber-stamp?

Where do members live?

What are important social contacts and relationships with other influential people?

VII. Merchandising/Retail:

Percentage of credit accounts in white community? black community?

How are credit ratings obtained? Who processes them?

How does institution operate — through mail? phone? over-the-counter?

Do people subscribe to receive product? to receive information?

Are blacks involved in granting credit?

VIII. Unions:

Does institution hire union employees? Is union discriminatory?

Is recruitment through union?

Apprenticeships available? for whom?

How does union bank? Who runs union?

(same questions apply to a union as to an institution in general)

How does the union relate to the black community?

Does the union have black stewards? black officers?

IX. What contributions are made to the community by companies and officers?

Contributions to the Joint Negro College Fund?

Programs to help house employees in presently segregated areas?

Contributions to NAACP Legal Defense Fund, community organizations in black communities, Urban League, etc.? Use of money and power in issues crucial to the black community?

X. Is there a company committee to develop and carry out a program for implementation of a nonracist policy?
(a) Company officers appointed to supervise a program
(b) Regular examinations of compliance with policies
(c) Education of all levels of management
(d) Persons appointed to relate especially to black services and suppliers

XI. What image is created by company?
Contents of bulletin boards?
Menus in restaurants?
Pictures on the walls?

SELECTED BIBLIOGRAPHY*

Black Consciousness:
Baldwin, James. *Fire Next Time.* Delta, 1963. (p)**
———. *Going to Meet the Man.* Dell, 1948. (p)
———. *Nobody Knows My Name.* Dell, 1961. (p)
Boggs, James. *The Negro in America.* Beacon, 1963. (p)
Brown, Claude. *Manchild in the Promised Land.* Signet, 1965. (p)
Cleaver, Eldridge. *Soul on Ice.* Delta, 1968. (p)
———. *Collected Speeches and Writings.* Delta, 1968. (p)
Cruse, Harold. *Crisis of the Negro Intellectual.* William Morrow, 1967. (p)
Douglass, Frederick. *Narrative of the Life of Frederick Douglass An American Slave.* Harvard University Press, 1881.
Drake, St. Clair, and Horace Cayton. *Black Metropolis.* Harper Torchbooks, 1962. (p)
Ellison, Ralph. *The Invisible Man.* Signet, 1965. (p)
Essien-Udom, E. U. *Black Nationalism: A Search for an Identity in America.* University of Chicago Press, 1962.
Fitch, Douglass. "Doing My Thing." Detroit Industrial Mission Article, 1968.
Frazier, E. Franklin. *Black Bourgeoisie.* Free Press, 1957.
Giovanni, Nikki. *Black Feeling, Black Talk.* Afro Arts, Inc. (160 W. 85th St., N.Y., 40024), 1968.
Grier, William, and Price Cobbs. *Black Rage.* Bantam, 1968. (p)
Haley, Alex. *Autobiography of Malcolm X.* Grove Press, 1964. (p)
Jones, LeRoi. *Blues People.* William Morrow, 1963. (p)
King, Martin Luther, Jr. *Why We Can't Wait.* Harper, 1964. (p)
———. *Where We Go From Here: Chaos or Community.* Harper, 1967. (p)
Lincoln, Eric C. *The Black Muslims in America.* Beacon, 1961. (p)
Marine, Jene. *The Black Panthers.* Signet, 1969. (p)

---

*A current annotated bibliography is available from People Acting for Change Together in Detroit, Michigan. A copy may be obtained by writing to: PACT, 163 Madison Avenue, Detroit, Michigan 48226. I also recommend asking PACT for David Snider's "A Story of Racism," which is an excellent interpretative bibliographical essay on racism. Also, "Bibliography on Racism" available from the National Institute of Mental Health, 5600 Fishers Lane, Rockville, Maryland 20852.

Washington, Joseph. *Black Religion*. Beacon, 1966.
Wright, Richard. *Black Boy*. Perennial, 1945. (p)
———. *Native Son*. Signet, 1940. (p)
———. *White Man, Listen*. Doubleday, 1957. (p)

Black Power:
Barbour, Floyd. *The Black Power Revolt*. Sargent, 1968. (p)
Carmichael, Stokely, and Charles Hamilton. *Black Power: The Politics of Liberation in America*. Vintage, 1961. (p)
Cleage, Albert. *The Black Messiah*. Sheed & Ward, 1968.
Cone, James. *Black Theology and Black Power*. Seabury, 1969. (p)
Killian, Lewis. *The Impossible Revolution? Black Power and the American Dream*. Random House, 1968.
Wright, Nathan, Jr. *Black Power and the Urban Unrest*. Hawthorne, 1967. (p)
———. *Let's Work Together*. Hawthorne, 1968. (p)

Black Power Examined by Whites:
Fager, Charles. *White Reflections on Black Power*. Eerdmans, 1967. (p)
Griffin, John Howard. *Black Like Me*. Signet, 1960. (p)
Hough, Joseph, Jr. *Black Power and White Protestants*. Oxford, 1968. (p)

Racism — General:
Alexander, Charles C. *Ku Klux Klan in the Southwest*. Kentucky, 1965. (p)
Ashley-Montagu, M. F. *Man's Most Dangerous Myth: The Fallacy of Race*. Meridian, 1952; 4th ed. 1964. (p)
Block, Edie. *A New Look at U. S. Investments in Latin America*. Radical Education Project (Box 625, Ann Arbor, Mich., 49107).
Brown, H. Rap. *Die Nigger Die*. Dial, 1969. (p)
Citron, Abraham. *The 'Rightness of Whiteness'*. Michigan-Ohio Regional Educational Laboratory, 1969. (p)
Editors of Ebony. *The White Problem in America*. Johnson, 1966.
Fanon, Frantz. *A Dying Colonialism*. Evergreen, 1966. (p)
———. *Black Skin, White Masks*. Grove, 1967. (p)
———. *The Wretched of the Earth*. Grove, 1966. (p)
Hernton, Calvin. *Sex and Racism in America*. Grove, 1965. (p)
Jordan, Winthrop. *White Over Black*. Pelican, 1968. (p)
Kelsey, George. *Racism and the Christian Understanding of Man*. Scribners, 1965. (p)
Kerner Commission. *National Advisory Commission on Civil Rights*. Government Printing; Bantam, 1968. (p)
Knowles, Louis, and Kenneth Prewitt. *Institutional Racism in America*. Prentice-Hall, 1969. (p)
Logan, Rayford W. *Betrayal of the Negro*. Collier, 1967. (p)
Memmi, Albert. *Colonizer and the Colonized*. Beacon, 1965. (p)
Mid-Peninsula Christian Ministry (2369 University Ave., East Palo Alto, Calif., 94303). *Institutional Racism in American Society: A Primer*. 1968.

Miel, Alice. *The Shortchanged Children of Suburbia.* Institute of Human Relations Press (165 East 56th St., New York, N.Y., 10022), 1967.

PAR. *Mass Media: A Racist Institution.* Detroit Area People Against Racism (109 E. Nine Mile Road, Ferndale, Mich., 48220), rev. ed. 1969.

Segal, Ronald. *The Race War.* Viking, 1967. (p)

————. *The Americans: A Conflict of Creed and Reality.* Viking, 1969.

Shogan, Robert, and Thomas Craig. *The Detroit Race Riot: 1943.* Chilton, 1964.

Silver, James. *Mississippi: The Closed Society.* Harcourt, Brace and World, 1963.

Smith, Lillian. *Killers of the Dream.* Norton, 1949. (p)

Stringfellow, William. *My People Is the Enemy.* Holt, Rinehart & Winston, 1965. (p)

University Christian Movement, Department of Youth Ministry. Packet on White Racism (Order: Mrs. Betty Pagett, Room 1303, 475 Riverside Drive, New York, N. Y., 10027).

van den Berghe, Pierre. *Race and Racism.* Wiley, 1967.

Witt, William. *Racist Myths* (About Africa and Africans; The 'Peculiar Institution'; The Civil War; The Era of Reconstruction; The Period of Reunion and Reaction). PAR, 1968. (p)

Woodward, C. Van. *Strange Career of Jim Crow.* Oxford, 1964. (p)

Racism in Industry:

Boggs, James. *The American Revolution.* Monthly Review Press, 1963. (p)

Ferman, Louis, Joyce Kornbluh, and J. A. Miller (editors). *Negroes and Jobs.* University of Michigan Press, 1968.

Killingsworth, Charles C. *Jobs and Income for Negroes.* Institute of Labor and Industrial Relations, University of Michigan, Wayne State University, 1968.

Marshall, F. Ray. *The Negro Worker.* Random House, 1967. (p)

Marshall, F. Ray, and Vernon Briggs, Jr. *The Negro and Apprenticeship.* Johns Hopkins Press, 1967.

Northrup, Herbert, and Richard Rowan (editors). *The Negro and Employment Opportunity.* Bureau of Industrial Relations, University of Michigan, 1965.

Pearl, Arthur, and Frank Riessman. *New Careers for the Poor.* Free Press, 1965.

Ross, Arthur, and Herbert Hill. *Employment, Race and Poverty.* Harbinger, 1967. (p)

Somers, Gerald (editor). *Retraining the Unemployed.* University of Wisconsin Press, 1968.

Sovern, Michael. *Legal Restraints on Racial Discrimination in Employment.* Twentieth Century Fund, 1966.

Wachtel, Dawn Day. *The Negro and Discrimination in Employment.* Institute of Labor and Industrial Relations, University of Michigan and Wayne State University, 1965. (p)

Race Relations:

Allport, Gordon. *The Nature of Prejudice.* Anchor, 1958. (p)

Bettelheim, Bruno, and Morris Janowitz. *Social Change and Prejudice.* Free Press, 1964.

Clark, Kenneth. *Dark Ghetto.* Harper, 1965. (p)

————. *Prejudice and Your Child.* Beacon, 1955. (p)

Conot, Robert. *Rivers of Blood, Years of Darkness.* Bantam, 1967. (p)

Goodman, Mary Ellen. *Race Awareness in Young Children.* Collier, 1964. (p)

Silberman, Charles. *Crisis in Black and White.* Vintage, 1964. (p)

Black History:

Aptheker, Herbert (editor). *A Documentary History of the Negro People in the United States.* Citadel, 2 vols., 1951. (p)

————. *American Negro Slave Revolts.* Columbia, 1943. (p)

Bennett, Lerone. *Before the Mayflower.* Pelican, 1962. (p)

————. *Black Power, USA* (Reconstruction 1867-77). Johnson, 1967.

Davidson, Basil. *African Slave Trade: Precolonial History.* Little, Brown, 1961. (p)

————. *Black Mother: The Years of the African Slave Trade.* Little, Brown, 1961. (p)

DuBois, W. E. B. *Souls of Black Folk.* Fawcett, 1903. (p)

————. *Black Reconstruction in America.* Harcourt, Brace, 1935. (p)

Elkins, Stanley. *Slavery.* University of Chicago Press, 1959.

Franklin, John Hope. *The Emancipation Proclamation.* Doubleday, 1963. (p)

————. *From Slavery to Freedom.* Knopf, 1957.

Franklin, John, and Isidore Starr. *The Negro in Twentieth Century America.* Random House, 1967.

Ginzberg, Ralph. *100 Years of Lynching.* Lancer, 1962.

Gossett, Thomas. *Race: The History of an Idea in America.* Schocken Books, 1963. (p)

Grant, Joanne (editor). *Black Protest.* Fawcett, 1968. (p)

Herskovits, Melville. *The Myth of the Negro Past.* Beacon, 1958. (p)

Katz, William. *Teachers' Guide to American Negro History.* Quadrangle, 1968. (p)

Quarles, Benjamin. *The Negro in the Making of America.* Macmillan, 1964. (p)

Indian History:

Brophy, William, and Sophie Aberle. *The Indian — American Unfinished Business.* University of Oklahoma Press, 1966.

Jackson, Helen Hunt. *A Century of Dishonor.* Harper, 1965. (p)

McNickle, D'Arcy. *The Indian Tribes of the U.S.: Ethnic and Cultural Survival.* Oxford, 1964.

Steiner, Stanley. *The New Indian.* Harper, 1968.

van Every, Dale. *Disinherited — The Lost Birthright of the American Indian.* William Morrow, 1966.

108

SELECTED BIBLIOGRAPHY

Miscellaneous:

Bradford, William Huey. *Three Lives for Mississippi.* Signet, 1965. (p)

Hazen, Nathan, and D. P. Moynihan. *Beyond the Melting Pot.* MIT Press, 1963. (p)

Hersey, John. *Algiers Motel Incident.* Bantam, 1968. (p)

Parsons, Talcott, and K. B. Clark (editors). *The Negro American.* Houghton, 1966.

Pettigrew, Thomas. *A Profile of the Negro American.* Van Nostrand, 1964.

Walker Report. *Rights in Conflict.* Bantam, 1968. (p)

Williams, John A. *The Man Who Cried I Am.* Signet, 1967. (p)

Wright, Richard, and others. *Black Voices.* Mentor Book, 1968.